Killing the Sky

ORAL HISTORIES
FROM HORIZON ACADEMY,
RIKERS ISLAND

NO. 4

Killing the Sky: Oral Histories from Horizon Academy, Rikers Island
Number 4

Copyright 2008

Student Press Initiative/Individual Authors

ISBN: 1-932948-42-2

Director, Student Press Initiative: Erick Gordon

Horizon Academy Collaborators: Josh Gray, Theo Figeroa, Ronnye Hightower, Charmaine McCants, Freebbie Rivera, Tanya Threadgill, Teo Torres

SPI Collaborators: Jondou Chen, Karina Kleiman, Kerry McKibbin, Vickie Ndibo, Giulia Suro and Lalitha Vasudevan

Cover Photograph: Sun Brockie
Cover Design: Chris Fazio, Jim Fenner
Layout Design: Jim Fenner

Photographs: Jondou Chen, Nicole Dickson, Chris Fazio, Jim Fenner and Erick Gordon

Editorial Assistants: Timand Bates, Lauren Bierman, Shelly Bingham, Jim Fenner Anna Himmelrich, Lauren Jenson, Greta Nelson, Sean Polka, Liz Thornton
Student Press Initiative/MCPET

Student Press Initiative/CPET
Teachers College, Columbia University
Box 182
525 West 120th Street
New York, NY 10027

www.publishspi.org

Acknowledgements

This project would not have been possible without the support and guidance of Horizon Academy's Principal, Ms. Gloria Ortiz and Deputy Executive Director of Programs - Department of Correction, Francis Torres-Mendelson.

Additionally, we would like to offer our thanks to Chief Patrick Walsh, Warden Emmanuel Bailey, DW Programs - Nathaniel Andrews, DW Security - Vanessa Singleton, DW Operations - Edmund Duffy, Sandy Roter - Supervisor of Instruction, Captain Ballard, Officer Edmonds and Officer Tomlinson.

At the GMDC-Annex, recognition goes out to Assistant Principal, Tonya Threadgill, Officer Roberts, teachers Ronnye Hightower, Charmaine McCants, Josh Gray, Theo Figueroa and family worker Mary Runyan.

Lastly, many thanks are owed to the officers, hard-working students and teachers at Horizon Academy.

CONTENTS

Foreword

Jondou Chen, Karina Kleiman, Vickie Ndibo and Giulia Suro

Jerry did not speak or move. With arms help tightly against his body, he guarded a small stack of photographs, snapshots from various locations around his neighborhood. A neighborhood on the outside, worlds removed from his present home on Rikers Island. As he struggled to hold back the solitary tear that came to rest uneasily in the corner of his eye, the other students sat quietly—contemplating their own pasts and the elation, surprise and remorse elicited by these pictures from home that told a thousand stories.

The setting is a classroom at Horizon Academy at the Rikers Island Jail in New York City—a school collaboratively managed by the Department of Education and the Department of Correction. Prior to this visit we had fanned across the five boroughs and into New Jersey, a group of four teacher-interns, following the written directions and hand-drawn maps provided by our students. Our task was to photo-document the places our young student writers had frequented while on the outs. We journeyed to empty amusement parks, corner delis, and bustling supermarkets. Bitter cold and through freezing rain, we encountered looks of bemusement and bewilderment from community members as we stopped to take photographs from our students' neighborhoods, gathering images to accompany the stories that you will soon read in the pages of this book.

At each stop, we found ourselves trying to envision what it would be like to walk down those streets with the student who had sent us here. For the past four months seven students had opened their lives to us through story, yet we struggled to imagine them in a context besides jail. We sorted through hundreds of photos from dozens of locations, wrestling all the while with the philosophical and physical divide that separated their world from ours.

When we handed each student a pack of photos, hoping they would acknowledge that we had captured their world outside the prison walls, murmurs of excitement rippled throughout the room. Some students flipped through the images in one mad dash, just to check how many they had, while others slowly fingered the surface of each photo, lost in thoughtful reverie. Jerry was initially the most animated, erupting with joy that we had brought him his 'hood. He enthusiastically showed his peers and then dashed down the hallway, sharing the photos with anyone he could find. Reprimanded for his disruptiveness, Jerry sequestered himself in the corner, where he whispered to himself, before becoming too overwhelmed to hold back the tears.

Much of the power of the Rikers Island Oral History project is evidenced in the symbiotic relationship between teacher and student and story. It is oft told, to the point of triteness, that the best teaching results in learning for both student and teacher, but in this instance it is genuinely true. The conversations we have had with our student writers over the past half-year and the profound ways that we have been asked to be empathic listeners, have led to deep examinations and a new awareness of the world in which we move. Moments of epiphany have occurred on both ends of the classroom and for this experience and for the power of these stories to reveal the world, we are humbled and grateful.

Introduction 1

Josh Gray

These stories have traveled far, carried like embers of last night's fire; protected, transported on the journey from there to here. Memories glow soft and slumber—awaiting the breath, the voice—waiting to be told. In dark times, night times, solitary times, the stories we carry with us warm and illuminate the islands of ourselves. They give meaning to our place in the world. As we give voice to our history, we stoke the flame of all those moments that have been burning unseen within.

Embers flame, and embers dim. Within these combustible pages are settled the charcoal-black letters of the printed word. As you read the stories of these young men, breathe a little of yourself into them. Their stories will rekindle, light, and flame. They are yours to carry with you.

The owners of the printed word become, too often, colonizers of history. Written history based on primary sources comes overwhelmingly from government documents, the press, and the holders of power in society. The histories in this book offer historians alternative and authentic voices of our age. By adding to the pool of primary sources from which history can be drawn, these young published authors have ensured that their story is not ignored, misrepresented, or forgotten.

They say history is written by the victors. With these spoken reflections, consciously molded and mended into artful forms, the men whose stories are collected in this volume tell their own stories in their own words. In doing so, they have become owners and victors of their history. Carry these stories with you. Protect them. Let them breathe, burn, fire, flame, and illuminate your world.

Introduction 2
Ronnye Hightower

As the ancient West African Griot passed along rich, family history and life lessons through oral tradition, so does *Killing the Sky, Number 4* provide the vehicle for our students to preserve and share their stories. The students at Horizon Academy, in association with the Student Press Initiative of Teachers College at Columbia University, began working together several years ago as a way to chronicle the major events in their lives.

This is the tenth year of Horizon Academy, a school born of a lawsuit that many thought would bear little fruit. The Department of Education and the Department of Correction forged a positive working relationship that has played a major role in the development of our school over the years. So we celebrate ten years of growth as a learning community. We do not celebrate ourselves as an institution, but we celebrate our students, who have benefited from the promise and realization of education. A promise that was unimaginable ten years ago on the desolate end of Rikers Island, the largest city jail in America, where school did not exist for 18 – 21 year olds. Most of our students hail from the five boroughs of New York City. Many of these youth decided to take paths outside of education and others are only a few credits shy of their high school graduation. Horizon Academy has provided an alternative venue where ironically, these students find the freedom to achieve.

The student writers were primarily chosen by the Horizon Academy staff and administration. The young men chosen to participate in this project have immense talent and potential. They are from diverse backgrounds, both culturally and socio-economically. Some were not avid readers, but still they wanted to participate in a book-writing project. Some were immigrants and new to this country. All of them are seeking the same opportunity: life, liberty, and the pursuit of happiness. And even though the students hail from these mean streets, you can see in their writing that they still have a desire to contribute to the well-being of their communities.

The oral histories presented in this volume tell of the lives—both tribulation and triumph—of our participants. They share stories that seek to offer a different path for those who might be heading this way. The storytellers want their readers to learn something from these narratives. The main theme of the writings, much like those stories told by the West African Griot, is that knowledge is power and with knowledge you can avoid the pitfalls of the Street. One of the writers explains his newfound belief that education is vitally important in one's life, and he encourages his young readers to learn from his mistakes.

The process of *constructing* an oral history is not an easy one. It requires long hours and diligence while writing and editing multiple drafts. The written narrative that results lets the world know that these young men exist, that they have important stories to be told, and knowledge to impart, that they have begun to embark on the journey towards fulfilling purpose in their lives. *Killing the Sky, Number 4* provides an opportunity for these young men to not only share their stories with the world, but equally importantly to say, "I AM HERE and I AM A WRITER."

The Streets of Harlem

Chapman

My name is Brian Chapman, I was born on January 25, 1987 in East Harlem in Mt. Sinai Hospital.

GROWING UP IN EAST HARLEM

We lived in the East River Projects, which is on the lower part of East Harlem and it's pretty much the same way now that it was back in the '90s when I was growing up, and the late '80s, you know? I still go over there and I visit and I still see crackheads and drug dealers and people getting hurt. You could always walk by and see drug dealers. I remember I used to come from school with my sister and we used to walk around and just look at people and think why they like that? They just scratching themselves, they look crazy. Their hair all messed up, don't look like they shower, they smell… and as you get older, you realize what those people were doing and why they was scratching so much. It was just the addiction. It was addiction to the crack or whatever they was doing.

Everything was pretty much like… I used to wake up hearing gun shots. There couldn't be a day where something didn't happen—either a fight, somebody got cut, somebody got shot, somebody got robbed. I remember this one time—this one serious time—I was about six, seven years old. I was walking… me and my mom, my sister, my mother's husband at the time, my brothers, and we were walking to see my grandmother, to go meet up with my grandmother at the bus stop at 106th. W were walking down 105th, going towards 1st Avenue. We were by the bus stop and some guy was just letting off shots right in the middle of the street He wasn't shooting at anybody, he was shooting up, just shooting… and I remember seeing this lady get shot, like, right in her face, and I stood there and looked.

My brother grabbed me and my mom grabbed me and we all started running back into the projects. I remember just seeing bullets ricocheting by my feet. My brother, Niko, he saved me that day. When the bullets were ricocheting everywhere, hitting the floors, I remember, he grabbed me and the bullet was no more than five inches away from my foot. He grabbed me and moved me just in time. I remember seeing that bullet just fly right next to me. I was scared, but I wasn't really terrified to the point where I was about to cry or something like that, 'cause this was normal. I think that was the part that's most sad for me… to be immune to things like this. Yeah, like, how could I be used to something like that? What kind of savage lives like this? Guess I felt that's when I thought we were living like savages. It scared me, but what could I do? It is what it is… something normal.

Growing up in Harlem is always going to be rough, especially if you wasn't raised around money or anything like that—and in my particular family, we were poor, you know. Most of us was on welfare, didn't have much, you know, but we made do with what we had. And it was tough because we didn't have enough money, like I said, to move around. We couldn't just pick up and leave whenever we want. We had to stay there, that was our only option. It was either stay there or be kicked out in the street.

THE MIDGET ROOM

Just this summer, a couple my friends died out there that I grew up with… and I be in here. I just be looking in the news and I be thinkin', "Yo' I wanna see something good." Like, I remember seeing a Harry Potter book release and I felt, oh, that's cool, everybody going out there, there's a big line around the block. That means somebody actually wants to read something productive, not something about drug dealing and shooting all the time. But then I look on the other hand, I see people I know on the news, you know? There's this kid named Joshua who died. He was a midget. He was born a midget, and I remember seeing this kid in the Boy's Club growing up. We used to be in what they call 'The Midget Room.' It's kinda weird. There was an age group from about nine to twelve—that was the age group in the Boys Club—it was called the Midget Room, and I remember playing foosball and pool with him, going to the pool, summer camp and all that, and then I look on the news and he's dead. Off a gun shot! And I'm like, who'd want to kill this kid? And then I sit back and think, like, he was selling drugs, you know? He was hurting people himself, even at his small size, you know, he was doing a gang-bang thing, so… it is what it is. It didn't make me feel anyway 'cause I was used to it. It was just like, another day there. Can't do nothing, if I want to get away from it, I gotta get myself outta the situation, like getting a better job or doing something to try get out, you know? But at the same time, I landed myself right back in here. You know, this about my third time here and I'm pretty much tired of it. This is the last straw.

Most of my friends, you know, they pretty much grew up the same way as me—poor, with nothing to really look back on and say, "Okay, that was good, I had a good time there," 'cause everything was horrible. A lot of them are just in here or dead. Some of them are here on the Island, I got some friends serving time in State, my boy just got hit with fifteen to life. I look back and I see why. This is just a pattern with all of us. Like they say, you know, you pick up on things you see. Grow up, seeing your mom or your dad on drugs or your dad going to jail, you gonna do that when you get older 'cause you think, that's okay. We all pretty much had the same lifestyle growing up since childhood, so they all just like me.

MY MOTHER: A STRONG WOMAN

What is there to say? My mother, she's a strong woman. She was always a single mom. She tried, you know? I can't say she was the best, she can't say she was the best. I feel bad sometimes, 'cause I feel like sometimes I made her feel like crap. I know there were times me and my mom were just arguing, I'd sit back and I say bad things like 'you wasn't good at this' or 'you wasn't good at that' or 'you always put this person in front of me' or 'you always put that person in front of me.' That was just me and my selfish ways—me just being selfish about everything. But I never sat back and thought about the good things she did. I always thought about the negative. I always thought about how she was using drugs. You know, before she could even pick up a book, she'd pick up drugs or something like that. My mom, she always hid it well, like, she didn't do it for months in my life. She did it for the early years of my life and after that then she stopped. She definitely hid it well, though. She never really did it around me. As I got older, you know, I started putting two and two together and then, stories start coming out. Everybody wants to open their mouth and everybody wants to tell me what it is or what they thought it was. I have a lot of family members that speak bad about my mom and then a lot of them that speak good about her. Everybody has an opinion. Can't really say nothin' about it.

Of course, I got angry with her plenty of times. I haven't always had the best relationship with my mom. It seems like the time when I'm at best with her is when I don't live with her. I haven't lived with her for a while now. When I'm away, and I'm living by myself, it's like we do better. When we together, we scratch heads. I guess our egos are the same.

My mom always tried, she'd always work a lot but she always made sure we had food, even if it was the littlest things. Like, I remember trying to eat just rice and eggs and that would be dinner for a whole week, rice and eggs over and over again! Nothing else—no meat, no nothing else, just white rice and fried eggs. That was just it, you know what I mean? We tried, but couldn't do much. Welfare wasn't paying us enough, jobs are hard to come by, especially with no education, and my mom didn't have much… she didn't even graduate junior high school, so she couldn't even do much. She had a baby at thirteen years old, and she wasn't ready to be a mom. She had my oldest brother then, so it was kinda hard for her. After that, she just never went back to school. She tried GEDs here and there and never made it out. I guess she just felt like it wasn't for her. I remember growing up, some of my family members used to act like my mom was the worst—she wasn't that bad. You know, she had her little faults, little flaws, but, you know, they was things you can't completely blame her for, 'cause she was just living off how she was raised and also things happened in her childhood.

I think about how sometimes, when she was upset, she tells us, "You guys make me want to relapse, you know you make me wanna go back on drugs. I can't deal with you." Then again, that's not completely helpful, but that was our fault, too. She's strong, 'cause to this day she's not back on drugs. Right now she's not working—she's really sick now, she ain't in the best of health right now. Not much I can say about her but that she's strong. She done other things, she got dirt, we all do… but it is what it is.

I CAN'T TEACH YOU HOW TO BE A MAN

My father, I remember a lot about him. Like, the way he looked. Exactly. My dad, he had this thing with these dark shades—he always had glasses on. The only time you'd see my father without glasses was when he was going to sleep. I think he showered with those glasses on! I always saw him with glasses. I remember he was a mechanic. He'd take me to Brooklyn, to my uncle's house, and I used to just play around him and he'd just look at me with this look in his face, like, "Ah, that's my youngest son and he's gonna be something." I think about it, look back at him, like, he wouldn't be proud of me right now, you know? He'd be proud of what I'm doing in here, but then, he'd look at it like, "Why'd you have to go to jail to go to school? Why'd you have to go to jail all these times—this is not the place you want to be." I remember he spoiled me like crazy. Everything I wanted, I used to get. I remember I used to cry and my mom would look at me like those tears don't mean nothin' and my dad would give her that look like, 'yeah keep on messin' with my son, you gonna get it.'

I really miss my father, miss having a strong male presence in my life. It's very important, having a role model. Yeah, that's a big impact on every kid's life that grows up without a father, especially boys. If my dad was alive today, for sure I wouldn't be in this predicament—one hundred percent sure of that! I would have never sold a drug in my life, I wouldn't ever have picked up anything, I would never have seen guns before maybe on TV, and I would never have seen Rikers Island, seen within these walls… instead, maybe just to come to visit somebody.

Like every mother will tell you—I can teach you how to grow up and be mature but I can't teach you how to be man. That's something a mother just can't do. She can't teach you how to be a man because she don't know how it is to be a man. She don't know what a man really feels or what a man really thinks in his head, you know, so I mean of course it's gonna be a big part of my life, why I'm locked up and why I've been into trouble so much. Of course that's one of the reasons, because I didn't have a father. That's only natural.

PS 146: MY ELEMENTARY SCHOOL

When I was about 1st, 2nd grade, kids don't want to go to school. Kids want to stay home, watch their Power Rangers, so I used to kick and scream going to school. My brother or my mom used to pick me up and drag me to school and I would still be kicking and screaming as soon as I entered the school. After a while, I'd calm down. I got older—about 4th, 5th grade—I started liking school… 6th grade, started liking school, little by little, I was just liking it.

Gym was my favourite course. We used to play soft ball, and I remember I had a teacher named Mr. Harris. He was the gym teacher. He was also in charge of a program they had in my elementary school called BBSP – Big Brother Sister Program. Mr. Harris—the leader, basically—chose kids from different classes, different age groups, and he'd have us monitor the hallways, or, like, stop fights in the yard, or whatever the case may be. As I got older around 4th, 5th grade, that was when he started picking kids from the classes, and I was one of the kids he chose. So, I started liking school, just 'cause I had a shiny neon orange vest and I thought I was cool, you know… no hall pass, felt like a cop or something. So I started liking school then, just because of BBSP and because of gym and playing softball. Yeah, it was fun.

And then, I got to junior high school.

MR. POPULAR IN JUNIOR HIGH

Junior High—I loved it! I was more into girls. Yeah, I was more into girls and there were so many girls walking around school and I was popular, you know? In junior high, I knew everybody, especially in my school because it was a big building right in the middle of Harlem, at 109th. It had about five schools in one. My school was on the top floor and it was called Harbour. They changed it a year after me being there, like, in my 8th grade year, they came… people put in the Academy for Performing Arts. I was involved in the band and I was pretty much one of the popular guys. It was a small school 'cause it was only one floor, but it would just be just one side of the hallway to another, and I was popular through the building 'cause I knew everybody.

Most of them dudes in the school lived around the area or I knew them from the Boy's Club or when I used to play in the Junior Knicks, something like that, you know. All the girls, like… growing up in certain areas, everything is about how you dress. You're popular on how you dress. If you don't dress a certain way, no matter how cool of a person you could be or how big and tough you are, if you don't dress a certain way, you can't be down with certain groups and you know, I was an average dresser. Jordans, just like every other kid around the area, Jordans, Northface, things like that… A little Timberland… I had those designer Mecca shirts, Pelle Pelle, things like that. I guess that's what made me popular, 'cause I dressed like all the rest of them I acted like all the rest of them.

The girls liked me, you know, even though when I was in 7th grade, I was a little chubby. In Elementary School and Junior High I was chubby. Then like 8th grade, I got slim. I made a transition and they were like, "Oh, look at him!" There were some of them who was feelin' me when I was heavy-set. A year later, I come back and I was skinny, so everyone thought, "Oh, okay," like a lot of the girls. I had my own little crew, my own little people I used to chill with, used to run around doing minor bad things like cutting school, you know… it was minor things. Wow, what wouldn't we be doing? I mean, there were cut parties we used to go to during the day time. Yeah, I mean, kids who'd have keys to their house because their parents worked during afternoons, so they're not going to be home to open the door so we'd cut school with them. About twelve guys, twelve girls, go to one house, party, do whatever. We'd smoke, drink, dance, music blasting. At that age, usually most of us were already sexually active so most of us were just having sex. The average ghetto teen, I guess… nothing more, nothing less.

We didn't really wild out too much, you know what I'm saying, until the end of the year.

STEVENSON HIGH SCHOOL ON PUGLEY AVENUE

My high school experience sucked. I went to Stevenson High School in the Bronx, yeah.

After a certain amount of years in the elementary school, about 4th grade, I moved to the Bronx. I was still going to school in Harlem. I went to elementary school and junior high school in Harlem while I was still living in the Bronx. So, I went to Stevenson High School on Pugley Avenue. Wow, there was so much crap going on at that school. Like I remember, my first week, a kid got stabbed in his throat with a screwdriver outside the school. Right outside the school. And I saw it! Like I said, it was something normal, things like that happened all the time, but it was like, damn, in high school, like, my first week? That's not something I want to see my first week of school!

He got stabbed with a screwdriver, right in his neck, at the entrance of the school. The building is so big that they had so many different exits, entrances, you know, and they had different kind of what they call the 'Sweep Team.' They had a crew of the Deans and security guards mixed with regular officers, police officers, and they'd go around the hallways, securing the hallways, securing all the exits and entrances. But there were so many exits and entrances in the school that they couldn't secure them all at one time. They were too busy chasing all the kids out the hallway, bringing them into one classroom, like everyone they'd find cutting in the hallway, they'd put in one class and they'd keep them there until the next period. Then, they'd export them all to the regular classes.

I was leaving school. It was about the middle of the school day and I was cutting school. School was over because depending on what grade you were in and depending on your credits or whatever, you have different time schedules. Like, seniors, they used to come in at a certain time and leave at a certain time. They wouldn't be there the whole day like we would be, and I guess this kid was a senior and he was just coming into school and I'm cutting, I'm leaving school.

I just walked out the door and saw the screwdriver in his neck. I didn't see him get stabbed but I saw the screw driver in his neck... he just laying there bleeding and I am like, "What the f--- is going, what's going on?" What kind of stuff is this, my first week of school! I don't want to see this. It kind of discouraged me from going back, but I'd go back and do the same thing all over again—Cut, cut, cut, cut. I never, I don't think I've ever been in school in Stevenson for a whole day and just stayed, from the first period to the last period. I don't think I ever did that. I think after lunch, I always left.

I'd go to cut parties, once again. But, see, high school, it's different than junior high school. In high school, you go to cut parties with other high schools. Like, I remember going to cut parties with students from Evander or students from Morris—those are all schools in the Bronx. They'd be just a bunch of schools in one house, and now it's not twelve boys and twelve girls anymore, now we got like 30 boys and 40 girls in a one floor apartment, lights out, flashing lights everywhere, like a real party. Drinking, smoking, always smells of weed in the air, smell liquor on people's breath, everybody was dancing, having a good time. I don't remember being in school one whole day in Stevenson.

After a while, I started getting into problems in school, fighting all the time. I remember I used to have, with this one group, I used to always have problems with them. Me and my friends were always fighting with them. Always, like in the hallways, no matter where we saw each other, we'd be walking through the hallways going to another class, there'd be a fight.

It started off with girls, then it just escalated on. After that, anything, like, you look at me wrong, we're fighting. You say something wrong, we fighting... even if you didn't mean it, you know, even if you weren't hinting it at me, if I thought that you was bringing it towards my way, we was gonna fight.

My mom, she used to get cards from the school—they'd send a card or call and say that we was cutting school. She knew I was cutting school. She knew and she'd be upset, but what could she say? I was gonna do it regardless. She'd tell me to stop, she'd tell 'Please don't do this,' 'Go to school,' 'Get an education.' Was I gonna listen? No! Was she gonna be there to watch me all the time? No! So it was what it was, I did what I wanted and she be doing what she had to do.

DEAN OF THE SWEEP TEAM

I remember there was one Dean in my school and he was a part of Sweep Team, the team of Deans that run around the school chasing us. And I remember he used to always be like, "Chapman, you're a trouble-maker." I'd act like I didn't know what he was talking about—you know, playing it cool. He'd say, "You're a trouble maker. I hear you, you think I don't see right through you? I see through that whole little game. I was young once like you. I'm a Latino just like you. I grew up in the same area just like you. I know you. I can see your character. You're a trouble-maker." He said "That trouble-making thing that you have going on is going get you into a lot more dangerous trouble. You gonna ruin your life for that." I remember he used to always come, every time he saw me in the hallway, "Chapman you are trouble-maker. I'm gonna wait, I'm gonna catch you doing something. I'm gonna catch you." I'd play it cool, like, "I don't know what you're talking about, man. You got the wrong person." And he started, "If I know you by name, this school has a thousand-something kids in it, if I know you by name, what do you mean, I got the wrong person? I know the whole (government) Brian Chapman, and you live this place, dah-da-dah, I know everything about you. I'm watching you when you think I'm not. I see y'all fighting in the halls, I see y'all running around, I see you leaving school. But you're gonna do what you want regardless, but as long as you're gonna do in front of me, me catching you, if I have enough time I'm gonna

Chapman

grab you up, I will get you."

But most of the time, he used to catch me like just out the door. He called my name and I start running. I'm up the block by the time he come out the building.

If he could see him now, I'd say that he was right. Like me, I got a real big chip on my shoulder. People used to tell me, you got a real chip on your shoulder. I never could be, I never could leave bygones, let bygones be bygones. I always had to be the person with the last word or be the person who did the thing the last. Like, if there was a fight, I always had to get the last hit, say the last thing to the person. I always had to spit on the person last. Whatever the case may be, I always had to do it last.

It's just my ego. I had a chip on my shoulder, thought I was a tough guy, that I was bigger and badder than everybody. But I got older. I look back now and there things in here that happen, you know... people lead you on and want to fight, people lead you to want to catch you and your case is going on.

Now I just sit back and be like I'm not gonna let none of that bother me. You can say what you want about me, think what you want about me, as long as you don't put your hands on me, we don't have a problem. I'm not gonna have that chip on my shoulder all my life. I got people out there who love me. I got a girl friend out there that I love very much. She's attracting me home. I've got a daughter at my house that I love very much, you know?

E-MONEY

I was doing a lot of foul stuff before I met my girl. Selling drugs, a lot of times I never used to buy the drugs. Half the time, me and my boys were just robbing drug dealers.

One day we needed money. We wanted to smoke, we wanted to drink. I remember the first time we did it, it was a Friday. It was about 7:30 in the afternoon, turning 8:00. I was bored, had nothing to do. We was already bad, we was already carrying guns and all that, nothing new. But I was like, how the hell can we get some money in our pockets quick, know what I'm saying?

Our thing was, we weren't into robbing pedestrians or regular people on the streets, 'cause you can rob anybody in the streets and not know what they have on them. Like, I pull out a gun on somebody and tell them to give me everything and they only have two dollars in his pocket—there are three of us, how are we gonna split two dollars? two dollars for one of us is bad, imagine three of us? Come on. So we just started thinking about robbing people who we knew had money, like drug dealers. Drug dealers always have money. So, we'd do some research on the person, like we'd rob a lot of people that we knew but we didn't mess with them, know what I'm saying?

There was this guy named E-money. Yeah… they call him E-money. You know, he was making bread, come home with at least two Gs a night and at the time two Gs seemed like a lot to us. That's enough to buy enough weed and cigarettes and alcohol for the week. We good, just chill out all day. We used to just sit there and watch him, smoking, just acting cool, he didn't think nothing of it. He always used to see us we smoking and chilling and just watching the whole routine. Seeing how he moves so that when we got him, there won't be no problem. We just investigate everything about him.

One day, we was like, "Alright, we gonna get him," and he was the first guy that we robbed, plotting and scheming. Crazy, man. There was about four of us, yeah. We ran up on him caught him going in the building about to serve his thing to the crackheads. We robbed him right in front of the crackheads, everything he had, all his drugs—he had about six Gs on him… took everything, to be honest. He didn't know it was us though, 'cause we had face masks and hoodies over us. We were small in size, so it had to be one of the young 'uns. So, after that, he didn't know who it was, 'cause we chilled with so many people and he didn't know which one of us it was. Out of all the people that we chose, he couldn't point out everybody. So, he left it alone, but he started watching us all. After that we just moved on, started going to other areas, watching other drug dealers, stealing and robbing from them.

MY GIRL, HELENA

I used to talk to this girl, right? Like, all was not serious between me and the girl. We never had any sexual intercourse or anything like that. No, it was just a flirting, making-out thing, kissing and hugging and all that.

When we're online, on the internet, on the local pages all the teens go to meet up... I'm online and one day she just start spying me—we just became friends. We was writing each other, from writing we went to calling each other.

I remember the day I went to go meet her for the first time ever, I was with one of my boys. We was driving to Massachusetts and I was on the phone with her, I'm like, "Yo!" You know what I'm saying? "I'm gonna come through and see you. 3:00 in the morning, I'm driving to Massachusetts and on the morning that I come back, I'm coming back on the same day, I'm gonna drop through over there and see you." She thought I was lying,

We was just gonna drop somebody off in Massachusetts. We was doing the drop-off thing, kinda drop-off/pick-up—drop somebody off and pick some items up, you know what I am saying? Got back to the city around 11:00 in the morning and so my boy, he left me in the Bronx. He left me in an area where I could take the 17 Bus to go see her. I went, I called her on the phone, "Yo, I'm on my way to your house." And she's like, "Whatever, I'm on my way to school. You fronting, you fronting, You ain't comin' over here." She thought I was playing. We was just friends at the time! I'm like, "Listen. Just stay right there, I'm gonna call you right back". I'm already half-way to her house. She thought I was joking! So finally, I find the building, even though I am not from that area.

The first day I met her, I went over there beading, you know, with my gang beads, whatever whatever, and I remember her saying while we're walking, she told me, "Listen, when you with me, you gotta take that off. You can't wear that around me. I don't want nothing to do with that." I respected that. I took my beads off and put them in my pocket. We walked, went to the park.

I remember we walked to Katonah Park and just stood there. We was just friends at the time. But I wanted more, she was on some, "Nah, let's just be friends, I don't know you too well". We've had thousands and thousands of hours of conversation on that phone and plenty of messages back and forth on the internet, but this was the first time of actually meeting. I wanted more from her 'cause she was fly, you know, shorty's beautiful.

I never thought I saw love at first sight until I met this girl, you know, she was... everything about her was gorgeous! Her personality, her smile, everything! Her body was fly, she was thick in all the right places so I'm like, yeah, I'm gonna get her. So I told her "Listen, we're friends right now but I want it to be something more. Mark my words, I'm gonna get you. You're gonna be my girl."

We were standing right at Katonah Park and I'm telling her all this and ever since then that's history, I've been with her ever since. She's my heart, man. She stopped me from doing all that crazy stuff. It's what she said. She basically threatened me and basically told me that if I didn't stopped all the bull crap I was doing, she'd have no time to be with me and we couldn't be together... All that dumb stuff—I was gang banging. She knew I was gang banging off the bat. I was beading, flagging hard, but I didn't want anything to do with that after I met her, but before I met her, it was crazy.

I was deep into it… the gang banging thing, I was robbing people, I was selling drugs. I was basically doing nothing positive. I was doing everything wrong.

After that, every time I went to go see her, she'd tell me something new, like "Listen, you selling drugs, you are doing whatever you are doing, you got to stop if you want anything to do with me, 'cause I don't need that right now. I done had drug dealers in my life, I done been here and there with that, I don't want that no more. Especially she's hard on the gang banger thing, like she really didn't want me doing that. And I made a choice. I made a choice… either go with something that's important to me, something that I'm starting to have really real feelings for or go with something that's meaningless, that's gonna give me a problem.

MY DAUGHTER

My daughter is two years old. She's an angel, man. I mean, that's the biggest thing that God has blessed me with. Like even while I'm in here, I stop and I think about, like, damn, that little girl is another reason why I changed everything. I changed everything. I speak to her on the phone, she come visit me. First time she speak on the phone, she had me crying, crying good tears… not bad things, good things. One time she told me on the phone, "Daddy."

I said, "What happened baby? You know who you're talkin to?" and she said, "Come here." She told me to come here and I felt bad, I was like… damn, I wish I could. And this is the beginning of when I got here. So it's like three, four months in, something like that, she had me feeling real bad. Love her man—she's one of the most important things in my life.

LOVE AND LOYALTY

To tell you the truth, to me, there is only two things which are more important than money, and that's the love you got from your loved ones and the love you have for them… and loyalty. The loyalty you get from them. Other than that, there's nothing else—its love, loyalty or money. Those are the three things basically that I live for. Money, because, you can't go, can't do much without it. Can't live, can't eat, know what I'm saying? Just for the basics. Yeah, plus there are other people who have their little life style and I have mine.

Love… everybody needs love. In some way, shape or fashion, they need love. If you don't got no love from nobody, you just gonna be cold inside. Everything about you is gonna be cold. And you probably ain't gonna make it past forty years old living like that.

I'm not gonna say I have one most important person in my life, but I'm gonna say I have one most important unit, they all work as a unit. That's my dream team right there—especially my wife and my daughter. Got girls that aren't my real sisters, they mean so much to me, too. Their mother was a blessing to me. They took me in when I had no place to go, a real blessing—Diana Nicci, Francois, Janet, those ladies wow, they done so much for me in my life.

And loyalty, that's a major one right there. You gotta be loyal. You gotta be loyal to your friends, and got to be loyal to your family. Like In my neighbourhood, they have a famous phrase, two famous words that people used to put together was n------love. That basically means the love you got for your n-----s, your crew. It was a time when you… ain't nothing like n------love, 'cause you alone, know what I'm saying? When you have love for the next man that's not really family and y'all just loyal to each other, just like that, and y'all just love each other that much and hold each other that much. There's nothing like that. Females come and go but your friends, when you have a real friend, they never leave you. In my experience, I've only had about two female friends like that, that I could really trust. Now I'm down to one.

Chapman

REFLECTION

Some things, especially like, the younger generation—younger than me, cos I'm young myself—but, I'm just hoping that kids younger than me ain't gonna have to go through what my generation went through. I have a lot of 'Old Ts,' what we call old timers. Old T dudes be like, "Yo, your generation is crazy, your generation is pushy". And I used to ask them, "What do you mean by that? And they used to tell me "Y'all generation, generation X, the lost generation. Y'all don't know what you all want to do with yourselves". "You're just wilding out all the time, hurting people for no reason. Just doing meaningless b---s---, you know". I remember they used to always tell me, "Y'all generation is twisted."

I don't want the next generation to be like us—in and out of jail. I been to the Fall Building, I've been in here—it's crazy in here! You see crazy things. Right now, I'm in a school dorm and that's the best thing I've done since I've been here, is going to school dorm. All the other houses I was in before this… crazy. I seen people's face get shot off, like, sliced off, fights going on. I mean, I've seen people fighting for jelly at breakfast time, real serious-like. Two dudes in my house, fighting over jelly and I am looking at them and I'm like you all just fight for the littlest things, it's nonsense! I just want them to learn that this ain't the place to learn. Don't be like us, man.

I wish we would have listened to the older people, heeded what they were saying, like… I don't want come to jail. I have two brothers that did major bids. To me, it's major. To other people, it may not be… but six to twelve years in State prison, that's crazy to me. I don't want to do that, know what I'm saying? I don't want to see myself doing more than a year, two years. I don't want to see myself doing no time, period, but if it had to be, I don't want to see myself going upstate for all them years, missing out on everything.

You know, my two brothers, they run upstate, one of them did about six and the other did about seven, seven and a half, something like that... eight. They used to always tell me when I used to go visit them, "Man I don't want see you in here. Do what you gotta do, go to school, don't come in here." I never sat back and I never listened to them. I never did. Now they both out there. One of them is back in here but one of them is doing good, man, and he tells me, when I speak to him on the phone, "Damn, man, I can't believe you locked up, like my little brother, my youngest brother, can't believe you're locked up again." Yeah, it bothers me. A lot of people used to warn me. I never listened. I was just hard-headed.

I haven't really spoken to my mom that much... been about a month. It hurts. I haven't seen her in a while. She used to come once in a while over here in the beginning. When I first got here, she was coming, once in a blue moon... but it's now, I don't see her at all. It hurts not being able to see her face. I just to know that we haven't had the relationship I would like to have. Like I told you earlier, I feel bad, because a lot of things she did, I always forced on her. I always used to throw in her face, like, "Oh, you wasn't a good mother 'cause you did this and that," and now I feel bad. I look back and I say, "Damn, I wish I had never did that to her," 'cause she cried. I know she cries. She tells me sometimes when she cries in my face and says to me "I know I haven't been the best mother and I'm sorry", and I don't want to make her feel bad, but it's just the anger that I have for her, you know? She put us in danger, you know?

SOMETHING POSITIVE THAT I DID FOR MYSELF

I guess I'd have to say going back, just dropping out of the whole thug-living type thing. Just getting out of the whole gang situation, selling drugs and robbing people, all that. I guess that's one of my greatest achievements. Just being able to sit down and think and say there's something better out there for me than this.

A lot of my homies felt betrayed, you know what I am saying? They was like, you

Chapman

know, "Man, how you could think about leaving us for a chick? Come on, like, we got that n------love, my dude, we's clear with you." So some of them understood and some of them hated on me like, "Yo, I ain't even feeling it—you don't even talk to me." Some of them don't even talk to me to this day. I seen them in the street and I say who are these dudes? We know each other since yay high, we was these regular bad little kids together. Now we adults… and they just walk past me like we never even met each other.

It hurts, but what can I say, you know? I had to do something to benefit my life. And if you can't see that—as my friend, you're supposed to understand that—if you can't understand that, maybe you not my friends. You can't be doing the same things. And if you knew better, you'd do better. And basically I mean by that, if you knew that there is something better out there for you, you'd do a lot better that what you are doing. Some people just don't want to change. They just want to stay with the same life style.

FUTURE

I want my own business. Don't know yet in what, but I know I want to be an entrepreneur. I know I want to be my own boss. I don't want to work for anybody. I want to be my own boss. I want to say I own something, not something owns me. That's exactly why I'm in the Horizon Academy.

An End
to Old News

J-Syf

My name is Jerry Etienne. People on the street call me "J-Syf." My birthday is June 18th, 1984. I'm 23 years old. I'm from Ghost Town/Brick City, Jersey but I was born in Queens NY, and I lived in Brooklyn for a little bit. Ghost Town/Brick City is on the borderline of Newark, New Jersey and Irvington, New Jersey. I live on the Irvington side. It's a low class neighborhood, you know? A typical ghetto. The section I lived in is called Hoodaville. That's on the west side of Newark and the south side of Irvington. The street I'm from, where I be on, is 18th Avenue and Isabella Avenue. I moved there back in there in 1990 from Brooklyn… been living there ever since. That's where I been, that's where I'm from.

I grew up with my family: mother, father, and brothers. My mom, you know, typical mother, always been around for us, take care of our needs, did everything right. My father did the same. I've got two brothers, one who's four years older than me, and a brother who's two years younger. But even though I was brought up in a good home, you know, I still was out in the streets making bad decisions. I never had… I never really had an excuse to be out on the street, 'cause I grew up in a family that taught us right from wrong. They was always around for us and provided for us. It's just that I got involved in the street at a young age and, you know, from there, I just got corrupted. Basically, I just got filled with a whole bunch of stuff that the streets provided, you know? I don't regret certain things that I did at the time. That's what I wanted to do and that's what I liked doing.

Up to now, from age thirteen until twenty-three, ten years of my life, I've been in and out of the system. I haven't been on the street for a year, not once. Getting' locked up here and there, doing city bids, state bids… between all that, not really doing much. I was hustling, robbing, stealing cars, smoking, drinking, and hanging out, and I always hung around with an older crowd, so I was doing most of the stuff they was doing.

TURNING POINT

I grew up in a good family, na'mean? They brought me up right. You know how your parents always tell you don't mess with people and people won't bother you? I used to always follow that; I was never a bad kid. I used to be a class clown, but that was about it. At school, I was always good. I never hung out, I was always exposed to street stuff but I never indulged in it. I never had a reason to.

The turning point in my life was when I was about eleven, twelve years old. One particular day in the beginning of the school year when I was in the seventh grade, a group of boys jumped me after school for no reason. Just for the fun of it, na'mean? Every day after school, I would just walk home. Basically, I'd either walk home, or I'd walk a girl home, something like that. But that particular day, I was walking with my mans and we was talking, I walked him all the way to his house and on the way back from his house, I seen a group of kids. There's always a group of kids, 'cause there's always fights and stuff like that.

I recognized some of them. Some kids were from my class and some kids were from the other classes. I see them every day, basically, and as I'm walking back, the crowd filled up the whole street so I had to walk through the crowd. I was smoking a Black & Mild at that time. This one kid, who I knew wasn't the tough type, I knew him as being the class clown, not the kind of kid to act tough. I guess one of the other kids put a battery in his back and told him to get at me or something like that. He was like, "Give me your Black and Mild." I knew that wasn't something he would normally say. He probably would've said, "Yo, can I smoke with ya?" He wouldn't just outright demand that I give him one. Not thinking about it, I just gave it to him.

From out of nowhere, somebody punched me from behind. I started getting jumped by a couple of dudes. It was more than one guy who jumped me, and there were about sixty, seventy people watching, mostly spectators though, you know? I never touched the ground, but I came up out of there out of the crowd and this guy I knew grabbed me. He had me by the collar like he was gonna punch me, and I just said, "Yo, let me go, let me go!" I kept telling him, "Let me go!" He ain't punched me, he just looked at me. And then he let me go. And then from there, that's when I walked to my house to do what I had to do, what I wanted to do.

That's just what some kids did around that time.. and you know, that changed my life. My mom always told me that if I ain't mess with anybody, nobody would mess with me. Here, on this day, these boys jumped me for no apparent reason. After I got jumped, little did those boys know I lived right around the corner from the school. I went home, and went to go get my brother's gun and come back around the school and shoot the dudes that tried to jump me. But in the midst of doing that, my mom seen me and started screaming and hollering, asking me about what had happened. I started walking out the house to go after the dudes, and that's when my brother and his friend came and rushed me, snatched the gun from me, put me in the car and told me to show them where the dudes were at. So it was me and my mom and my brothers in the car drove around the corner to the school where we jumped out and we started attacking the boys that jumped me.

From then on, my life went downhill, you feel me? After that experience, two guys that didn't like the guys that jumped me came up to me the next day after school. They had seen what was happening to me and they was the guys that told them to stop jumping me, they were the guys that really broke up the jump for me or whatever. They came up to me and said, "Yo, what's up? Do you wanna start a little clique?" Na'mean? So I'm like, "Why not?" Before I got jumped, I would have never thought of that, never thought about joining any little gang… but after that happened, I thought might as well 'cause this could have happened again at any time for no reason again, so this way, I would have some protection. Not only for protection, but so I could be a part of something.

Our gang turned out similar to what they was doing, the kids who jumped me. Every day after school, we used to just beat people up. Now, it wasn't ordinary people that we knew wouldn't fight back. It would be tough guys, the dudes that jumped me; we used to go at them all the time. People who claimed they was tough, we'd go at. Then that evolved into something that originated at our school—we took to other schools. Over a period of time, our gang went from being four people into being twenty to thirty people. We went from school to school, fighting kids and recruiting people. Things got really serious when our names started being out there. The police came to our school one day and sat the main people in the gang down in the principal's office and told us that any more incidents and we'd get locked up for gang-related crimes.

I was twelve going on thirteen.

ALL DAY ON THE BLOCK

A couple of months went by, and as a result of me being in that gang and hanging with them dudes, the time frame between twelve and thirteen, that's when I started everything, all at once. Being in that gang opened a lot of negative doors for me. When I was hanging with them, I used to smoke here and there, but I started smoking weed. You know, I started hustling, stealing cars, robbing people, na'mean? All that started for me at once – hanging out, drinking liquor. All day on the block, stuff like that.

Drinking and getting all involved, that came with being in that clique. Most of the dudes in that clique looked at me like a leader. I kinda seen myself as a leader too, 'cause I used to be the one that looked forward to it. Every morning, I got up, I got the n----s together. That had me slacking in school. I used to cut school all the time. School was okay, I guess. I was doing good in school. It was just that I didn't find it important at that time. We had this older dude who went to the high school, and we used to cut school, go to his house every day, and just chill, smoke, drink, have girls over, things of that nature. And being in the gang for those couple of months, we were in the papers as being menaces to our area. Even after school hours, we used to just rob people, stick people up that was walking in the street, stuff like that. It didn't matter if they was grownups or young kids. Steal people's cars, stuff like that. We was in the papers and the cops had all of our names and pictures and they wanted to lock us up and stick something to us. One day, we went to the high school and we jumped some kid and I got locked up for it.

I didn't get locked up for that long, na'mean? I was locked up for probably about three weeks or a month. Then I came home, but my mom, she was already mad at me 'cause she found out I started smoking and drinking and doing bad in school. So she was like, 'You know what, I have to get him outta here.' I'm Haitian, by the way, I grew up in a Haitian family. And she was like, 'You know what, I can't take this no more, I'm gonna send you back to Haiti for a year so you can change your life, and you'll see all the struggles that are going on over there so you can come back and leave all this stuff alone.' But it ain't really turn out the way she wanted it to.

THIS YEAR THERE'S GONNA BE A BIG CHANGE

We got to Haiti, I'm there for a week, we chillin'. My mom's like, 'We're about to go to this school.' I'm like, 'School for what? She like, 'A school you can go to.' I'm like, 'Nah, I'm not going to no school.' That whole week she pleaded with me to go to that school. After a couple other family members talked to me, you know, I'm like, 'You know what? Forget it. I'm here now, so might as well.'

J-Syf

At the time I used to hear how Haiti was: poverty, people getting killed, all that stuff. But I had visited Haiti when I was younger a few times on vacation. I didn't want to stay, but between the times me pleading going to the school and you know the place I was going, I seen different. It was only certain areas that was in poverty. Like the main capital wasn't in poverty. I seen cars that I see over here, a lot of different things, you walk into stores like you do out here, buy stuff. It wasn't like I pictured it to be, some place in the woods with no electricity, no society.

Anyway, I signed up for the school. I looked around the school campus and it was all right. So I came back from the school, and my mom said she was leaving in a week. I'm like, "I already know. I heard you talking to the pastor on the phone, talking how you were gonna trick me, I already know." They left me out there with her sister and her brother, my uncle, and I was living with them. I turned fourteen that summer.

So I'm just sittin' there at their house thinking about what am I gonna do. So, you know what, she wanna leave me here, I'm just gonna take advantage, take it as a learning experience… something like that. So I told my uncle, like, "Come on, you gotta teach me the money rate exchange and all that and where to go buy certain things—where to go change my American money for Haitian money, where to go buy clothes, where to go buy food, so when you're not around, I can go do it by myself." You know, where the basketball court, soccer fields at, places I would want to go enjoy by myself without you always having to be around. And within a whole month, I say middle of July to middle of August, he showed me all of that. It didn't take long for me to learn the currency, how the money was and all that. I knew how to travel, get around in taxicabs and little motorcycle cabs, how to get from city to city, town to town, and all that, so I started liking it.

Got to the school at the end of August. On August 20th, school starts. At the school in Haiti, you only get like a month, a month and a half summer vacation. You go to school about ten and a half months. They go up to fourteen grades, not twelve grades. So, it was time for me to go to school—went school shopping, got my clothes ready, we had to wear uniforms but I was staying on campus on school. They had dorms on school grounds. The name of the school was the English Adventist Academy of Haiti. That's one of the major private schools that they got for people who had money to pay for their children to go to school. Ain't no free schools in Haiti. Well, there probably is some, but the majority of schools in Haiti you have to pay for. So, I went there on the first day of school. I got to know some of my roommates, people in the dorm. Most of them was people like me: their parents sent them down there for a change. We had some people from Brooklyn, from New York, from Boston, from Miami, from North Carolina, from all over… their parents sent them there to make a change for themselves.

The same mentality I had up here, I took over there. Some kid that was there the previous year was telling us about how there's this little off-campus gang that goes to school. They had two schools, the French school and the English school. The English school was what we went to, and the French school was what the natives, they went to. They had people who lived on campus and people that lived off campus, so they had a little off-campus gang that one of my roommates was telling me that, 'Yeah, every year they always mess with the girls,' the American girls—American meaning Haitian-American, who come to the dorms every year. And they don't get the chance to mess with them, this that and the third.

This year, there's gonna be a big change. Me and my other man from Brooklyn, Stretch, we tell all the other kids in the dorm there's gonna be a big change. I don't know where you come from but it don't go like that. We're not gonna take none of that. So we formed a little gang. And like we said, we got the girls that was in the dorms. We was messing with them. Each of us had a girl we was messing with, and the n----s that the other kid was telling us about, you know, from the start, they knew that we was gonna be a problem 'cause they see how we used to always walk around in a group. We already had the girls locked down, we tried to start knowing people on the campus area, the females that work in the cafeteria, the security guards that work at the posts, the president and stuff like that of the campus.

Several events took place on that campus throughout my time there. First event that happened was the guys that was off-campus got jealous of not being able to get the girls from the campus. One day, like, three months into the school year, coming from watching the soccer game to go to the cafeteria to eat, one of them said something slick about my man's girl. Talking about a girdle, like, "Oh, why his girl not wearing a girdle?" But he said it in Creole. My man turned around and said, 'What? I'll beat you up.' I'm telling him leave it alone, leave it alone, leave it alone. Some crazy s--- went down… I don't know

One night, a whole bunch of college officials came and raided the dormitory and found all these weapons and they kicked out a lot of students—mostly people I was messing with from our little gang. I didn't get kicked out 'cause I was kinda like, doing good at the same time. I was really starting to find myself spiritually while I was there at the same time, you feel me? I was reading the Bible. The campus was Adventist, really based on church and church ways, and we used to go to church services and I would make little sermons about my life, testimonies about my life, and read the Bible and things of that nature. I was really starting to find myself and the counselors and the people that headed the dorms was noticing that, so they took a liking to me, regardless. They knew about my little beef with the other guys, but some of the other guys I was associated with that lived in the dorm, they had the wrong type of attitude. Like, they would be disrespectful to certain officials, and they'd get caught cutting class. I got caught cutting class too a couple of times, but nothing major. But anyway, that was just one of the major events.

FRENCHIE

The second major event—well, the last major event that I got into there—there was a rule on the campus after 9:00, everybody got to be in their dormitory. My mans was playing basketball on the court and the security guard came and took the basketball. It was 8:00, it wasn't 9:00 yet, but he took the basketball and went back to the security post with the basketball. My man was like, yo, he wanted his basketball, so he went to the security post to get his basketball. I'm at the dorm at this time. So he tried to get the basketball, but the security guard don't want to give him the basketball. So he started to get angry and the security guard seen it and got scared and grabbed his shotgun so in the midst of my man trying to get his basketball he went to go open the gate of the security guard post to pull him out and the security guard shot him in the hand. What made it even worse was that he played the piano for the church, you know? He wasn't a bad guy, he went to the French school, and he wasn't a bad guy at all, basically. He didn't smoke, he didn't drink. He was involved with our little clique, but he wouldn't get into all the negative stuff that we were getting into, that the American kids was getting into.

When one of the little kids came back to the dorm and told me, "Frenchie got shot, Frenchie got shot!" I'm like, "What!?" I heard the gunshots go off, you feel me, but I'm thinking they just chasing away people, 'cause they have thieves that climb the walls that come on campus and steal things so they shoot at people like those. I ran out there and ran towards where everybody was at. All the girls was out there, people was out there, and I see Frenchie on the floor all hurt. I'm like, "Yo, what happened?" He just hollering and screaming and I'm like, "Yo, what happened? What happened?" And everybody was saying that the security guard shot him and I was like, "Hold up!" I went to the security guard post and I'm like "Yo, why you shot him?" cursing him out in French and English "Why you shot him? Why you do that? Why don't you come out here, why don't you do that to me?" I did the same thing my mans went and did and went to go open the security gate and when I did, he shot.

The pellets from the shotgun hit the bars of the door and fragments from the pellets went in my eye, and that knocked me out. Next thing I know I woke up in the hospital, and next thing I know from that, I was being put on a flight back to Jersey. Well, back to New York, LaGuardia, 'cause my mom said she didn't want them to do the operation and take the fragments from my eye down there 'cause I would've lost my eye. It wasn't that life threatening, but I could have lost my eye, so I had to do it up here.

I really didn't want to leave, you feel me? Because I was there for New Year's, I went with my cousins who took me to Undeo, where my mom was born. It was the part of the country where you got little Haitian villages. They still live in huts made of straw and mud. It was like a life-altering experience for me 'cause I still see how they comfortable still living like how Indians used to live back in the day or early people. I slept there and it felt good. It didn't feel like it was poor. I knew they was poor, but it didn't feel like that to me. It just felt like regular, every day life, you feel me?

I experienced a lot of different things, been all over the country. So I didn't want to leave. I was being treated good. My mom sent me money every week, na'mean? I did a lot of stuff. So I really didn't want to leave. But I came back, they did the operation, and chilled for a while. I was still fourteen.

CHANGING LANES

Back in New Jersey, I picked up from what I left over there and I started right back again. I got back into a gang, not with the same n----s that I ran around with before I went to Haiti but some Haitian cats that live around my corner. They already had a gang out there. I was running around with them, getting into fights everyday after school. I already had a reputation from middle school and everybody heard about me getting sent to Haiti, so there was a lot of people in the high school already knew about me and I didn't even know them. I just picked up where I left off, still got into trouble, getting locked up more frequently. I had a choice... I just chose to be in a position of power.

UNTOUCHABLE

But I liked what I was into at that time. When I was in the little clique I had after I got jumped, I liked drinking, smoking, chilling on the block. I liked having the power that other people was scared of me 'cause they knew what I was capable of.

One time, I was at high school and most of the Haitian kids that was in the clique, the ones that was younger than me anyway, looked up to me, like one of the head n----s that was about my age. And one day, I was one of the heads that was there, that was supposed to be at a gang fight, about to fight against some Crips, and I'm standing there in the front line with one of the Crip dudes in front of me and the rest of his people behind him and the rest of my people behind me and I'm standing there, looking in his face. So there's a lot of arguing going back and forth... There was some crazy fights back then.

BLINDED BY THE STREET LIFE

My father passed away when I was eighteen, and that's when I really started slowing down and taking a good look at life for what it was. I still was getting locked up after that, but I wasn't involved in all the stuff I was into, like going around beating people up. I was robbing here and there, but I wasn't doing it on an everyday basis. I slowed down a lot with all the stuff I was doing.

My dad, he was a good father, na'mean? I can't complain nothing about him. He always took us out. He always took us to family members' houses, making sure that we knew our family. If he was going somewhere, he'd always ask either me or  my little brother if we wanted to come. I always wanted to go, 'cause I liked to see other places instead of where I was living at. We used to go everywhere, like New York, Pennsylvania, Boston, state parks for family picnics, Coney Island, Great Adventure. He always provided me with money, if I needed it, when he had it. That's basically it.

My father smoked cigarettes. I didn't know that he smoked weed. One time, he's like, "You wanna go fishing?" I ain't never been fishing with my father before and this is like a year before he died. And he says, "You wanna go fishing? All right, let's go and s---." So we went to a park that had a lake for fishing, and we was fishing, we was sitting in the car, getting the gear ready, and he pulled out a bag of weed, and that shocked me. He knew I smoked weed but I didn't know he smoked weed. He was my father, and Haitian parents, stuff like that, you just don't tell or do around. Or any parent, really, that care about their kids, you feel me? Anyway, we got the fishing pole out, smoked, just talking about stuff, life and s---. And that's really the only father-son moment that we ever had before he died. You feel me?

I was eighteen when he passed away. I was at the house. What's crazy is that I kinda had a premonition. I had a dream three days before that he died, that he was gonna die. You know, I was so caught up into the street life that he was in the hospital for a month, two months, and I only went to go see him once. That still hurts me to this day that I was so caught up in the street life, like, I always had it in my head like he gonna be alright, you feel me? Even when I had that dream where he died, I still didn't take it seriously. I told my mom, "Yeah, I had a dream that father died." "You should go see him." But I ain't gonna see him, and when he died I felt like I got shot 'cause it hurt me so much. I know I should have been going to see him while he was in the hospital. And even when I had this dream I still didn't go see him and now he died and I can't tell him the way I felt.

It was around that time I really started sharing my feelings with my parents, you feel me? Well, that was the beginning of sharing my feelings with my parents or with anybody, telling them what's on my mind, what I'm really thinking about. I wanted to do that before my father died, and he died and I didn't have a chance to do that, and I caused a lot of pain in his life. For me, from being in the stuff I was in, he didn't want that, he didn't want me doing certain things. My mom used to always blow it up, rub it in my face that oh, it's 'cause of him, I died… and that held a lot with me, even though she would say it just to get me to try to change my life. She didn't really mean it, but still, that hurt me a lot, hearing her say that.

When I was nineteen, any time I'd come home after I got locked up she'd give me this speech and say my father died because of me and 'cause of me, she's gonna die from stressing. She used to always say that, even before he died: "You gonna kill us from stress." And I was too much into the street life, na'mean? I love my parents with all my heart, you feel me, but I was just caught up in too much of the wrong things. When I turned twenty, that's when everything hit home. Like, I started seeing everything for what it was, everything my mom

J-Syf

used to tell me. I should have took all that and kept it, ran with it, but I didn't. I was listening to friends. It was my decision, too, but I just didn't. I don't know, man. I was blinded by the street life. Blinded by it.

When my father died, I wanted to change my life and stuff like that. And when my son was about to be born, that made it even more serious for me, and that was when I just dropped everything. You know what I mean? Up to that point, I just got into life... Ain't gonna say much, but you know, I'm in the situation where like I have to see how the outcome goes, you know?

MY PRIDE AND JOY

And now, I got a one-year old son. Now, I really stopped everything. Robbing, stealing cars, fighting, shooting and selling drugs. Everything. My son was born August 24, 2006. Before he was born, in the beginning of the summer 2006, I just stopped everything: stopped hustling, stopped hanging out, stopped hanging with all the friends that was not influencing me but opening doors for negative influence to come upon me, to do what I was doing. I stopped hanging out with them, I started focus on having a family.

Ever since seventeen, I wanted to have a child. Before I had my son, Joshua, before my current girlfriend, my ex-girlfriend had two abortions. That's one of the main reasons her and me broke up. This time, when I knew my current girlfriend was pregnant, I was happy, but I was scared at the same time, 'cause this time I knew it was going to be for real. With my ex-girlfriend, the second time she was pregnant, I was like, she's just gonna have another abortion, 'cause that's what she did the first time. She didn't really want to have a child 'cause she was worried about what her parents, what her family was gonna think. My current girlfriend, she didn't care about what her family and other people would think, and I knew it was going to be for real this time. Before I got happy, I was scared 'cause I didn't know if I was gonna be in a situation like this, being locked up, when he was born or before he was born. I didn't know if I was going to be able to be a good father. I didn't know. I was scared of a lot of different things.

I found out in January 2005. I was home and me and my girl friend was talking on the phone and she was like, she missed her period again. I'm like, "Again? When was the first time?"

"In December."

"Why you didn't tell me this?"

"'Cause, I wasn't sure, I thought I was just late."

"So you think you pregnant?"

"I think so."

I'm like, "Go get a pregnancy test and find out." So later on that week she did, she took it and it said she was pregnant. So I'm like, "Go get another one, just to really make sure." She did—and she was pregnant. When she told me, when we talked about it the first time, I was hoping she was, you know? But after I knew that she was for sure, I just started thinking about a whole lotta stuff, like damn, I'm finally about to be a father, na'mean? But at the same time, I don't want to be a bad father or, you know, a father that's never there, get caught up in some b---s--- that had me in jail for life, so I'd never be in my son's life. And I was just thinking about all those different reasons and that's what made me scared. As time progressed, I got over the fear–but not really. 'cause, you know, I heard that within the first three months of a child being born is the most critical, 'cause some babies die within that first three months, like from heart failure, even in pregnancy... and that's the only time I was scared, after me getting over the first couple of months. After that, I did all the things that fathers are supposed to do while she was pregnant. I was taking care of her, making sure she was making it to all her appointments. I was still getting locked up in between here and there, but no long bids. I got locked up twice during her pregnancy, for two weeks, three weeks, matter of fact. But I made sure I was there for my son's birth.

I really stayed with her, went out with her, went places with her, took her out to eat, just put most of my time into her, until all the way up to the time of the birth and I was there. Got there. She went over her due date, na'mean? We were supposed to be August 11th but it was August 23rd. We went to the hospital but that was the date they said she had to come to hospital. They was going to induce her labor and I stayed with her. I stayed overnight and the next day, they induced her labor, broke her water and all that. I was there. I watched from beginning to end. That whole time, I was there. You know... the first couple of months after my son was born, I don't know why, even though I seen him physically... I still couldn't believe that I was a father. I just couldn't believe it.

I was holding him one day and I kept saying to myself, "I'm a father? I'm a father?" Like, nah... I'm just holding him in my hand, looking at him, saying, "I'm a father..." I kept saying it, I must have sat there for ten minutes saying that, not being able to believe, na'mean? He right there, looking in my face, just smiling, and that just right there made me. I had to give the street life up. I had to. Not even hang around on the block where I was at, 'cause my neighborhood always been a red zone. The FBI had that area under investigation ever since

I lived there, checkin' up on the drug business. So, it was like, I could walk to the store and get locked up, you feel me? It's just that serious out there. I could walk to store and get shot, you feel me? That's how serious it was out there. Looking at him, I was like, yo, man, I gotta move from where I'm at, 'cause that right there could have me missing my son's life. Someone might end up killing me, I might end up killing somebody, end up in here for life. My son, that's my turning point in my life. There was three major turning points in my life… good turning points… well, not good … three major turning points: The day I got jumped, the day my father died and the day my son was born. Na'mean?

FIRST CHAPTER OF A NEW BOOK

I tell my story when I get the chance. I like being a mentor. Kids in my area that I see that I know are going down the wrong way, I can tell them about my life. I tell them, "Yo, you do this, you end up in a bad situation. I know teachers will tell you but take it from me. Yeah, you see me out here hustling every day, you see me out here sticking n----s up, but I already got too deep into it for me to just stop it like that. You still young." I'm talking to kids like eight years old. I know a kid right now, eight years old, he steal cars and drives better than me. He can barely see over the steering wheel and is getting chased by cops every day, and he escapes. And I be tellin' him now, "Yo, this not what it is. All you n----s need to stay in school, go to school, pick up a sport, something like that and just stick to it, and at least get your high school diploma and decide what you gonna do from there."

I always instilled that in my younger brother, because I ain't never wanted him to end up on the road that I went down. Then I would feel that my mom, my parents, would have blamed that on me, 'cause he do look up to me in certain ways and certain things he picks up from me—but the positive, you feel me? None of the negative. That he smoked, I can say he got from me, but any other negative thing, he don't get from me. You feel me? So all the little kids in my area that I'm close to, even when I see them doing things that are going get them in trouble, I pull them up. I'm like, "Yo, come on, man, don't even do that. You know you're supposed to be in school. If you gonna cut school, don't run in the street." I'm not encouraging, but I just trying to tell them, so they don't end up in the situation where cops are gonna have to come and question his mother. I see a lot of kids like that get put in the system, 'cause they see

that their parents or their mothers don't have control of them. In my area, most of the kids, their parents are either crack-heads or they don't have jobs. They just livin' off of the city, the state or whatever. So, there's a lot of that in my neighborhood. In Newark, Irvington, East Orange, all them places.

I got bigger plans for myself right now. I'm trying to go into business for myself. I've had jobs, and jobs is not me, especially I'm too used to... I did the drug game, you feel me? What jobs is paying nowadays, I can't even stay at a job. My first job was at a Country Club, valet parking. I wasn't even supposed to be parking cars. I lied on the application and said I had a license. I knew how to drive, but I was fifteen, parking cars at the Country Club. The second job, I was working at Boston Market, and from Boston Market, I did construction here and there. Most of the time, I was doing construction, but with Boston Market, then I was working at ShopRite, and between all those I was doing construction. That's what really held me down.

When we came from the projects, the Vandemeer Projects in Brooklyn, to a house in Jersey, a two-family house, but it was a house, you feel me? And there used to always be little repairs needed done around the house. My mom always needed painting to be done, basic stuff that I would see on TV and stuff that was easy. I could always do it. Then, when I started the construction on the real, one of my neighbors across the street had a brother who did construction, doing it for fifteen years and he taught me damn near everything—how to paint correctly, put up walls, put up beams, how to build rooms in basements, how to put floors down for ceramic tiles, linoleum tiles, counters, put counters in, sinks in. I know about plumbing. I know about electrical, putting in windows, replacing windows, roofing, siding of houses, vinyl siding for houses, masonry, putting bricks in, cementing on the floor, putting gates in, landscaping, grass, how to put in lawn. He taught me things that went into depth, such as cabinet making, aluminum siding. He taught me all of that.

Sometimes, I wish I never got into all that stuff, na'mean? All the violence, getting beat up, stabbed, hit by a car, et cetera. If it wasn't for that, I could have probably continued doing construction, you know, on a consistent basis. I like doing construction.

I do a lot of things that average black person, average hood person wouldn't do, I'll say it like that. Construction-wise, I know that when tasks has to be done, job has to be done, I ain't gonna stop until I finish it. I won't take no lunch break, no nothing. I like tasks like that. I like designing things—landscape design, architectural design and things like that. As far as recreational things, there are a lot of forests in Jersey and stuff like that, wooded areas. I like taking walks, nature walks and stuff like that. I like animals, I like scenery, I like boats, things that an average kid that grew up in an urban neighborhood wouldn't be into, you feel me? I write poetry, na'mean? I'm just into a lot. I'm a thrill-seeker, too. You feel me? I want to go skydiving, want to go deep-sea fishing, deep sea diving, things of that nature.

But back to construction: I really didn't stay with it too long 'cause at a certain point my body started wearing down. Because I been injured so much. I been in about six life-threatening car accidents, and I crashed my brother's motorcycle. I got jumped a few times by groups of kids, 'cause I was involved with a gang, and they caught me. I got hit with baseball bats, clubs, you know what I mean, stuff like that. And all that wore and tore at my body. In construction, you gotta deal with a lot of heavy lifting and stuff, so at a certain point I would wake up and my body would be in excruciating pain. I had to take pills until I'm like, "I can't do this no more." So I'll go back into it, you know, but I won't be able to stay for long until I find out what's really wrong with me, 'cause I ain't ever really go to a doctor.

Anything that ever happened to me, after I got jumped or cut, or stabbed or something like that, I never really got to go to a doctor to check up on myself. Most n----s won't, you feel me, unless they get shot and they're bleeding. Some n----s I know, you just get shot, just wrap it up, leave the bullet in there, you feel me? That's not something n----s around my way really do, go get checked up. I'm gonna do that though, see if I got any loose joints, broken bones. Life was hard in my area. Life was real hard. Any ghetto, wherever it's at, be it New York, New Jersey, California, Florida, wherever, that's how it was.

Like right this morning, when I woke up, I felt pain, you feel me? When I woke up, you know when you wake yourself up, when you lift yourself up, I couldn't. When it rains and stuff, it always happens to me. That's how I know I have problems in my body. I hear from other people too, like that got hit by a car, certain injuries to their body, certain times when it rains, they have pains in that part of their body. That happens to me, but it happens all over my body. And I have to lay there for a good ten minutes until I just fight the pain and just get up. And then once I start moving, like right now, my body still hurts, but I've been moving so much, I'm not even thinking about it. You know? That's how it is. Every time it starts raining or if I injure myself, all over my body, it just hurts.

I don't regret some of the things I went through, 'cause without them I wouldn't have the knowledge that I have now and the way I am. Cuz now, when I talk to my mother, I tell her what's on my mind. My mom, I know she notices a big change from back then to now 'cause now I talk to her like she was a sister. I tell her everything, every little detail that's going on with me, what I talk about with my girlfriend, like she's a friend, you feel me?

I talk to her and my other family members, too. My little cousin, especially. This experience, me being locked up right now, brung me closest to my little cousin. She about to be nineteen this year, and she's always been a quiet and secretive, secluded, she kept to herself, especially about serious things that happened in her life. I never had a sister. I always wanted a sister-figure, and when I was locked up, matter of fact, I wrote to my aunt and I guess my cousin must have got the letter and read it and she wrote me back, telling me how she felt. In the letter, I was basically just telling my aunt how I messed up my life. I should have did this, I should have did that, I should have listened, and I guess that must have touched my little cousin and she wrote me back. She didn't know that I could be so open like that. And she wished she could be open like that, and I wrote her back saying, "If you need somebody to open up to, I'm the one." She told me she never knew but I always tried to get into her life ask things about her, but she always blocked me out 'cause she thought I was being over protective cousin or whatever. But when I explained it to her in the letter, she started to understand. So now, I see a big improvement. She's telling me a lot of things about her life that she never told anybody and she only tells me. Not even her parents, not even her friends, only me. Everything.

She's another main focus in my life. I'm trying to be in her life like a big brother, 'cause she has an older brother, but he's caught up into his own little world and even though that's his sister, he's not worried about her like that, like I am. So, she holding me down while I'm doing this time right now, with letters, just exchanging thoughts and feelings and what's going on with our lives, getting to know her and she's getting to know me, just keeping me relaxed while I'm here. Helping me not to stress out a lot, basically.

I hope whoever reads my story, man, they could just take it as a lesson, like even though they probably didn't go through the same things I went through. I'm a standup dude. All that drug game, all that negativity in life, it's not worth nothing. It's not worth a dime. You gonna have fun for a while, until you hit that dead end and it's like… damn.

You feel me?

Situations of a Motherless Child

D-Rock

ALLOW ME TO INTRODUCE MYSELF

People call me D-Rock. I'm twenty-one years old, and I was born on November 13th, 1986 in South Jamaica, Queens. And right now, I consider Washington Heights my home. This is a poem I wrote called, "A Slow Death."

Standing here, behind these bars

Days and night, passing by

Inmates making my bid real hard

At times I find myself, praying to God

Asking for strength to survive another day

Now I walk around in a haze

Looking for a way to hide the pain inside

But tears start falling from out the sides of my eyes

From all the messed-up things I've seen my brothers doing to my brothers

Some of the same things the whites did when their faces hidden behind white covers

Why do we hate one another?

Why do we sell drugs to our baby mother's mother?

Ain't selling drugs just another way of committing murder?

A liquor store on every corner... and you wonder why your mother's never sober?

Your little brother's running around with no coat in October, so you become the man,

and come up with this plan, to get some money and take care of the fam

Now you're gettin' money so school's on the burner because

You're too busy robbing and stealing just to get by

You see your life going nowhere so you go and get high

Hustling to live but wantin' to die.

D-Rock

Writing poetry helps me to express my feelings and it also helps me pass the time.

GRANDMOTHER

I grew up with my grandmother. I have four brothers and five sisters so there are ten of us and we all grew up together in a two-bedroom apartment so it was crowded. We started off in South Jamaica, Queens on 118th and then maybe eleven years later we moved to Washington Heights.

My grandmother was real strict, a real strict lady. She was raised down South so she was real strict. She didn't have time to look after all of us, so me and my two older brothers was always out in the streets. She really

concentrated on my sisters 'cause my mother had a drug problem and wasn't in the picture that much. So me and my brothers would be out all night, but when we'd get in the house, we'd be in a lot of trouble. We would get beat a lot. We grew up holding a lot of resentment against my grandmother because it was like she cherished the girls more than the boys. It was rough. We always had terrible arguments and disagreements, but she tried, for the most part.

A lot of the disagreements was about how everybody else got to go first, like the girls got to go first, or about the hand-me-downs. I didn't like wearing my brothers' clothes 'cause everybody in the projects know that they was my brothers' clothes and so we got into a lot of arguments about that, and about school things because I didn't learn as fast as the other kids.

She'll always consider me a slacker, like I don't try, but even if I did try, it's harder for me to pick up things like other kids. It was a problem 'cause she felt like I wasn't going to school to learn. She felt like I was going to school just to play around. So we argued about that a lot.

NO FOOD IN THE HOUSE

Eleven years later, when I was about eleven years old, we moved to Washington Heights to be with my mother. It was a two-bedroom apartment... all ten of us, a dog and my cousin. It was real hectic. And that's when I started getting into a lot of trouble. I started hanging out with the wrong crew, with all the hustlers and the older people and I started going on the wrong path but in a way, I learned a lot of street smarts, you know. I learned how to survive. Hanging out with them kinda helped me 'cause three years later my mother left us again so it was just me, my brothers and my sisters. We had to take care of each other. So for me, learning from them helped me take care of my family. I'm not gonna say it was the honest thing to do and yet it was things that would help me get food on the table, take care of my brothers and sisters.

My oldest brother, Anthony, he's a nerd. He's in college, he's doing things. He's real good with computers but he really didn't help out that much 'cause he was always into his books and stuff. My other brother, Aaron, he was a clown. He liked to have fun and play around and everything, and then there's me. Then there's my sister, Christina. Now my sister Christina, she was the neat freak. She kept everything clean, that's what she did. But she went to school. Erika, my other sister, had two kids and was at home with the kids and that also made it hard. Basically, everyone else went to school. So it was only me and my other brother Aaron who wasn't in school, trying to take care of family. There were a lot of fights, lots of disagreements, lots of arguments, and the same thing... hand-me-downs. Nobody wanted to wear the hand-me-downs.

What I learned from growing up is how to survive. I feel like it made me stronger, 'cause now I know what it's like to take care of a family. And now I know how important it is to have an education. That's why I'm here, to get my education because if I had an education—instead of doing the other things I did—I could have got a job and do things the right way, take care of my family the right way instead of me going out there and doing all these mysterious things and ending up in here.

I learned to take care of my family about a week after my mother left and there was no food in the house. Nobody really knows the story behind why my mother left. I think it's because she's still fighting with her drug addictions. So we just came home from school one day, I was out all night, and they come from school and I got there first. And I see she not there. I didn't think nothin' of it. I thought maybe she's out shopping or whatever and then my sisters and brothers started coming home from school. And two days later, I'm like "Where's mommy at?" She was gone so I don't know. After that, it's like we all had to depend on each other. I was fourteen, and there was no food in the house and so I'm standing there and I'm like, what am I going to do? My little brothers and my little sisters, they crying, they hungry. I'm like, what am I going to do? And yet, I see my next door neighbor. He always have money. He don't go to school but he always have money so I went and ask him "how do you get all this money?" And he tells me, "I mow a lawn here, I wash windows here and pack bags at Pathmark" so these are things I started to do so that kinda taught me to work to get my money. After a while, I started robbing and stealing to get money.

When it was at its worst, we didn't have nothin' to eat. Out of all the money we scraped around in the house, there was maybe three dollars. All we got was a whole bunch of chips and junk food. And that was basically all we could get. I kinda felt ashamed having to knock on neighbors' doors, begging for food. I'd say, "Excuse me, me and my brothers and sisters don't have nothin' to eat and was wondering if you could help us out with anything." We was in the projects in an apartment building. And, gratefully, there was a Spanish lady and she had leftover food that she was going to throw away that she gave us. Oxtail, rice… it was good food. So I was thankful for that but that was one of the worst times.

I felt like the most important thing was for me to help my family eat and make sure they're in school. Even though I wasn't in school that was something I stressed for them 'cause I didn't want them to have to go through the same things I went through. At first, it was just every day sandwich meat, you know, from the deli… turkey and ham and cheese and bread because that was all I was able to afford. But then after a while, I started picking up more things and I started raising prices and building a bigger clientele. So, after a while, it stopped and it was franks and beans and then maybe it was rice and meat. One of the best times that I fed them that I felt I did a good job was on Thanksgiving because, as time grew, I learned how to save money, how to open a bank account, start paying a little bit, put a little in the bank. So on Thanksgiving, we had a turkey. We had pies, sweet rice, yams. We had a nice Thanksgiving. All of us cooked. We did our best. All my brothers and sisters… it was a family effort.

Most of the time people would come and go but I always tried for the whole family to be there for one meal. But most of the time, when the family was there, it was at the soup kitchen around the corner at the church. I remember exactly. They served at the church at 5:30 so I have to be getting everybody up, trying to get the little ones washed up and get everybody dressed so that we all could get at the church around the corner at 5:30 so we could eat dinner. A lot of times we made it and a lot of times we didn't, but the people at the church started to get familiar with us and they actually started helping us, giving us extra food and stuff. So we had a lot of help from the community.

STRUGGLING

I went to 202 for junior high school. Now I got into a lot of problems because I was slower at learning than other people. It kinda bothered me because I was like, how come they can get it so fast and I can't? I felt bad for myself. How come I can't learn this? So I didn't focus as much and I started goofing off because I couldn't understand the work. And so, I struggled the whole way through but I made it through junior high school and into high school. Now high school… I don't know how I made it, but I made it to the 11th grade before I dropped out of school and it was hard. It was real hard but I'm happy I did it, that I made it that far. That's why I'm in here now, inside the H, trying to finish.

During junior high school, I noticed everybody in the class knew their times tables except for me. They knew from one through nine and I only knew my two, three and my five times tables. That was kinda hard during every math class because they would move on to fractions and all these other things and I'm stuck on multiplication, you know, because I don't know multiplication so the fractions and everything is too hard for me. So that was kinda hard because then I felt like I was singled out. My desk was on the side, in the corner, and I'm doing one thing while the whole other class doing another thing so that kinda made me feel like I was an outsider.

I remember my junior high school math teacher, Miss Thomas. She was a real heavy-set, dark-skinned teacher and she wouldn't give me no attention during class. She'd give me work and put me in a corner. The class had about twenty-something kids in it and the desks were maybe seven in a row, going back, and my desk would be on the side by the window. So I'm facing the wall while the rest of the class is facing her desk. It was like I was in my own separate area. She would say to me, "This is what you need to learn," and then she'd give a lesson to other kids so we didn't really interact because I'd be over here, doing the work she gave me and all she'd do is tell me what I got right and what I got wrong. She wouldn't explain it or show me how to go about doing it but yet she'd go, you gotta find out how to do this.

The other kids in the class were essentially nice. The reason why I understand my times tables now is because of a girl named Amanda. Amanda, she sat down next to me like one day out of the blue. She just came and put her desk next to me and sat down and said, "Here, let me help you." And then she started going down the times tables, showing me easy ways to remember and just showing me how to go about it. Amanda, she helped me get through that math class. If it wasn't for her, I wouldn't have passed that math class. I don't know to this day why she came over there to help me. Maybe she liked me or something. But I'm grateful for it. We kinda lost contact after that math class.

I was surprised that I made it to high school because I struggled so hard and felt like maybe because I wasn't on the same level as the other kids, I wasn't gonna make it. I felt like I was always two steps behind. In any reading class, my reading wasn't good so I kinda figured I got the social promotion—you know how they got this social promotion—because I interacted and I did participate in the class. But I was sitting in the back so the teacher wouldn't see me so I wouldn't have to read out loud because I knew I wasn't able to read it. But I did comprehend it.

I put myself in the back so the teachers wouldn't see me, so I could sit there, slouched back and I could listen because I could comprehend the words but I couldn't read out loud.

In my high school English class, we was reading a book, Scorpions by Walter Dean Myers. It's a good book. So I'm in the back and I don't even have the book open. The book is on the desk and I'm just listening and then, out of nowhere, the teacher looked at this sheet and she called my name and told me to read the next three paragraphs. I couldn't. Then she pulled me to the side, she asked me, "How did you make it all this way and you don't know

D-Rock

how to read?" She was being serious because she pulled me to the side in the hallway and my response was that I understand the work but I just can't read it. No teacher really called on me to read out loud. Then she said she was real surprised and she put me inside a smaller class. Up to that point, I was hiding from the teacher… from everybody. When she called me to read, I was nervous. I didn't want to read and I didn't want the kids to make fun of me 'cause I couldn't read so I had a lot of feelings. I was scared, nervous. Even in the next class, they wasn't as advanced as the class I was in but they was still ahead of me. So when I got there and they had to start me off with the vowels and with sounds and with certain words make certain sounds, the class made fun of me. But I kinda learned to deal with it over time.

My brothers and sisters have asked me several times, like, why you always yell at us and make sure we go to school and you didn't graduate? And I tell them, I didn't want it to be as hard for you all as it was for me.

BENCHES

This older guy lived in the neighborhood. He would always sit me down and tell me, well I see you trying real good for your family… what about you? He said, you got to better yourself to be able to help somebody else. There was no relationship between us. Tell you the truth, I'm not sure if I even know his name. He was one of the old guys who would sit on a bench and drink. You know how you got the old drunks who would sit on the bench. He was short. He had grey hair, kind of a bald head in the middle. He walked around with a cane. He had a

pigeon feather in his hat and we was always sitting on the bench and drinking with the older people on the side. And he used to always pull me to the side and I'd go 'cause I respect my elders and if he had something to say, I would listen. So he used to tell me a lot of experiences that he went through and relate them to the things that I'm going through and it was always funny because this guy, I never really seen him a lot but the stories he told me, I could always compare it to what was going on in my life.

When my little brothers and sisters didn't like wearing hand-me-down clothes, he would tell me a story about how his parents used to get clothes from the church and give it to him and stuff. And they'd go to organizations, the churches and the Salvation Army and all these places. I'm thinking, last week my little brother James and me got into an argument 'cause he didn't want to wear the hand-me-down clothes and now this week, out of nowhere, he came up to me and tells me that when he was younger, his mother used to do this, his mother used to… so I kinda took that. And this church sponsored two of my brothers and two of my little sisters. There's a Yogi Bear truck would come around and teach the gospel to little kids. It was at the Yogi Bear Church there was this lady, Nana. She got my brothers and sisters sponsored so they got clothes and school supplies and went to summer camp so that kinda helped out. And I got all that just from him, from the guy on the bench telling me that one story. So I try to take heed to the older people 'cause they know what they're talking about 'cause they been through things in their life.

Me and him, we talked for maybe two years. It was like this on and off thing. I could walk by and I could say hi and he won't say nothing, maybe not remember, but one day he'd be like just, "Young man, come here, let me tell you something." I stopped seeing him because I became too busy then I started going to Bellevue Hospital. I was participating in a Youth Group there and talking about some of my problems and getting some things off of my chest.

So maybe I was busy a lot with my brothers and sisters and going to the program and trying to hold the family together.

THERE'S MORE TO LIFE

I grew up in Dyckman. That's where we are right now. It's a big drug area. There's a lot of drug traffic, so I try to teach my brothers and sisters that's not the way to go. We used to go to the big park to watch the basketball games. Dyckman used to hold basketball tournaments there. Some times, stars would come by. Like, Cam'ron came by. DipSet came

by like, right up the block. We used to hang out there, watch basketball games there in the summertime and also go to Inwood Park. There were little hiking trails in the park. We used to go on hikes, used to pack book bags with sandwiches and food and stuff and we'd go on hikes through the park and have a little picnic, find a nice spot, all of us. Used to be fun.

But the neighborhood, it's not a good neighborhood. There's a lot of shootings and stuff and basically I'm trying to teach my family just because you live here in the projects, you don't have to act like these people. You don't have to do the things these people do. There's more to life than that.

I had to learn that on my own because I learned that as much as I stayed in the projects and hung out with the people I was, that was how I'd get in trouble. The first time I got locked up, right? They wanted to hold up a store and they wanted me to be the lookout guy, and I was standing there at first and I'm like alright, I'm gonna do this because I was thinking about the money… like, let me get this money to take care of the family. But then, as I was standing there, I wanted to leave 'cause I was like, if I do this, I'll wind up in jail. Which I did. How am I going to help my family there?

Just like now. I was sent in here for reasons, and my family lost their apartment. My family is in shelters right now so I feel like if I wasn't in the street life, I would have done things differently. If I had just thought things out before I was so quick to do things, right now I'd be out there to help my family, take care of my family, other than in here. The neighborhood had a lot to do with it. I hope that my family can learn from this experience. Be careful who you call your friends 'cause everybody not always your friend. Try to go outside the neighborhood and meet people other than sticking with the same people, doing  the same things, 'cause those the people you see on the corner every day when you go to school. They on the corner when you come home from school. They on the corner. Why would you want to interact with people like that? So that's what I try to teach them.

THE ONE SHOT DEAL

Welfare was paying half the rent, and after a while I was receiving Social Security so I paid from Social Security. It was only like two hundred fifty dollars I had to pay out of my pocket. I didn't start paying rent until maybe two, three months after my mother left and then housing stuck a note under the door saying that we owed all this money in rent. It was this white piece of paper with the housing logo on it. It said how much money we owed and if we ain't paid it within a two month period, we'd be evicted. It was in the thousands 'cause I guess my mother wasn't paying the rent.

Living in the projects, there are things you hear. I'd be in the elevator, and I hear like the older people talking about yeah, "Well I went to Welfare, and got a one shot deal. They paid my rent." Just by listening, you actually can learn a lot. So I'm sitting on the bed, crying and thinking, "What can I do, what can I do? I don't want my family to be homeless." And so, it just came to me. What was the elevator lady saying? Something about a one-shot deal? About welfare? Let's see how that's going to work. So, the Welfare office is maybe four or five blocks down from the projects so I walk in and then I'm waiting on this line. Everybody is looking at me! Everybody. Like, what's this little kid doing on the Welfare line? So I get to the window and I try to explain to the lady that we can't pay the rent. She said, "Do you have some kind notice or something?" And then I gave her the note. I said I heard talking about a one shot deal for how we can pay the rent. She explained it to me. After she explained it to me, she's like how old are you? And I told her. I'm sixteen, about to be seventeen. And she's like, no. I was actually fifteen. So she said, "You need to have someone eighteen or older." And she was telling me, like, where's my mother and everything and I didn't answer. I just walked off the line. I went back home and I got my brother to come in and stay 'cause I already knew that it can happen and, yeah, they will do it for that one time but you gotta be of age.

They paid the rent and, after that, I started cleaning windows and doing this and going to the bodega. I sweep the bodega and they pay me for cleaning. All over the neighborhood… just to help out, doing whatever I could do and if people—a lot of people in the projects, the older ladies and stuff—if they wanted help, I would go to their houses and help. I'd go shopping for them, like they have a shopping list I'd go shopping and they'd pay me. So from little odds and ends, I make it. I paid rent for five years. Just about six years. Not including this year.

WHY ME

My oldest brother, he didn't really do anything. He was in school and when he wasn't in school, he was out on the couch. He didn't do anything. He wasn't motivated. I guess he was going through his own problems or whatever inside. My second oldest brother eventually got up and he had a little job and everything. But him? He took care of himself. He didn't really take care of my other brothers. He didn't look at it as, I'm the second oldest? Let me help out and take care of the family. He didn't look at it like that. He looked at it to take care of himself. He had the newest clothing and newest Jordans and stuff so he went through his money. But me... I felt like somebody had to step up and take care of the family. If they wasn't going to do it, then I had to.

When my mom left, I noticed that both of them are sitting there and my youngest brother was seven at the time and crying because he's hungry. I talked to my older brothers about it and it was a dead end. I was like, "Aaron, you got a job, you getting money, how come you can't help out? Help feed the rest of us?" And he's like, "Oh, well, go get a job. I'm taking care of myself. I got a job for me to take care of myself." That's exactly what he said... I'm gonna take care of me. He worked at Ellis Island. He was doing one of the food... in the kitchen or something like that. And my other brother, he didn't have no job or nothing. He just went to school. But eventually he did get one at a bar in Queens so he started helping out. Especially with my sister winding up getting pregnant for the second time, like, he really started helping out. Before then, before he started helping out, I just felt like somebody has to do it 'cause it had to get done... seeing my little brother crying because he hungry.

When my mother wasn't around, my grandmother always taught us to never see nobody hungry. Even though it was ten of us when my mother was around, our friends hung out with us and when they were hungry, she'd always make a way so that they would eat, too. So that was kinda how I was raised. I don't want to see nobody hungry so to see my own baby brother crying for food, I couldn't take that. I knew I had to do something. Right then, something told me, was here's where you have to grow up. Here's where you have to go out and provide.

The apartment was very small. It was two bedrooms, one bathroom, a living room and a kitchen. My three older sisters had the back room and then the three youngest had the other room and me and my brothers slept in the living room. We had a dog named Sandy and it was just real hectic, especially in the morning when everybody would get up and go to the bathroom and get ready for school and everything. It was always hectic. Having only one bathroom was one of the worst 'cause you got somebody in the shower and you got somebody using the bathroom, somebody brushing their teeth so you got to make sure you get the girls in there first 'cause, you know, they take the longest to get ready in the morning. I woke everybody up. I set my alarm clock for 5:00. Just like now. I'm programmed now to wake up at 5:00 'cause I was so used to my routine. 5:00... here, wake up Christine, Erika and April. You all are first. And then I'd wake up the little ones, and get them ready. Nay-Nay, Jo-Jo, Tee-Tee and James, I'd get them ready and get them out the house. After that, I walked them to school. By the time I'd get back, it be time to wake up Anthony so he could go to school...

They always would give me a lot grief like you not my father, you not the boss of me, who left you in charge? And I'd always say, I'm your older brother. I know I'm not your father. No, I'm not your mother, but I'm your older brother and I'm going to make sure that you do right. I'd try to tell them that, no matter what happens, you all represent us. I tried to keep them dressed nice because it was no secret to the rest of the projects that our mother wasn't there. They knew we was living alone. It was not secret, everybody knew. We knew everybody knew. You know, it even got to the point when one time somebody called up DCYF (Department of Children, Youth & Families). But yet, we beat it because my brother was old enough. But when I said they represent us, I mean that when you leave the house, make sure you dress neat, make sure you don't get raggedy clothes 'cause once you step out the door, you represent the rest of the nine of us. And I got to tell each of them. Try to carry yourself in a certain way. They see you out there.

I would try to make sure I gave them at least two or three dollars in their pocket. Don't go out begging. Try to have a little respect, a little decency. Whatever they did with the money was up to them. Up to them. You going to school, you stop and get your snacks or whatever… I'd try to give them that 'cause as long as they good, I don't care. As long as you go to school and as long as you take care of what you gotta do in school, whatever I can do, I'm gonna do for you to the best of my ability. That was me. If you asked them the one thing I stressed, that was school. That's it. That's all I wanted… go to school, get an education 'cause then you'll get a career and you'll get a good job and take care of yourself. That's all I wanted. Everything else, clothes, whatever, don't worry about it 'cause I'm gonna do the best I can to get it for you. My sister, she started babysitting and my brother, he started doing little odd jobs like me like mowing people's lawns, he would sell waters on the curb. I started to notice that they was getting their own little hustle going and that's good 'cause obviously they see me out here working. I don't got a job job, but I'm out here doing this, doing that, you know, doing all the odd jobs and they started to pick that up. So that's when I really started noticing that I am an example to them.

When my sister told me, my sister Erika, she told me, like, I'm not gonna be home until 7:00 because I got to pick up Miss Nicky's kids and I'm gonna babysit them. Okay, I said, maybe this is just a one-day thing but I started noticing it was every day and I noticed she was babysitting more kids and more kids and I started thinking. Then I saw my little brother James maybe a week after that, he started selling waters. He saved up his money I was giving him everyday to go to school with, and then went to the Walmart right behind the Pathmark. So he bought a whole big case of waters and he's selling waters now. He brought ice in a bucket and he's out there, selling waters to cars going by, and I didn't even know that until I walked by and seen him. He was twelve. And he was out there selling the waters and stuff so I just looked and I smiled. That was like a joyous moment to me, that they learned how to take care of themselves. They learning. And they wasn't stingy with their money like my other brother. They actually helped out with the little ones. I really took heed to that and I sat down and I was watching how they all started working together. Like our own community. I took great pride in it. I did. To this day. Even though I'm in here and the situation with them ain't so great 'cause they couldn't keep the rent up. They in shelters right now yet I hear that they still looking out for each other.

A HAND IN THE FUTURE

I know I really didn't have a childhood. I was forced to grow up so fast. I learned along the way. It was a big learning experience. And there's still lots to learn. Lots to learn. What I want to do now is, I want to learn how to run my own business because I want to open up a youth program. I want to own my own building, my own business for the youth so that people going through things, like the things that I went through in my youth, I can help them out.

I can spread that information, spread the knowledge so they can get into programs so I can help them. I realize that there's a lot of people going through the same struggles that I went through so I'd love to have a hand that I can reach out and help.

"Left On Our Own"

Sometimes, I feel like a motherless child,

Left in this world to survive on our own,

Now I stand up and make her kids my own,

Feeding and providing, trying to make a house a home,

Got into it with the law, because criminal things is all that was known

Now I dot my i's and cross my t's

Sitting in Rikers Island, trying to get my GED

All because of doing criminal things to feed my family

Left on my own,

Sometimes I feel like a motherless child.

A Lost Life
Now Found

Boy Slaughter

They call me Boy Slaughter. I was born in Roosevelt Hospital in Manhattan, New York on January 6, 1985, which makes me twenty-two. I've been raised in Harlem about half of my life, and the other half I've been raised in Brooklyn, so I'm kind of Brooklynized now. My family recently moved to Rochester, upstate. I'm settled. I'm kind of settled into going back up to Rochester.

SACRED MEMORIES

Harlem is just a beautiful place—growing up with a lot of parks. Clean parks, much cleaner than Brooklyn. Central Park was mainly the park that my mother took the whole family to. It's a park I enjoyed. You know, we had picnics by the lakes, we seen ducks. It was just so beautiful. Those are the sacred memories that I remember. Brooklyn. I would say Brooklyn was a rougher life. A real hard, rough life. Black people in Brooklyn struggle more, hustling, and a lot of gang banging activities. Accomplishing things is hard. Choices get made when people are neglected in society. I guess in general just living in the projects is different. Like walking to school in rough neighbourhoods—you walk by a corner and there's drugs and gangs.

My family was on welfare, feel me? And we didn't really have much. And that's one thing that made it hard for me. There isn't that much opportunity, when you're inside the projects or growing up in the projects, 'cause you hang around with cats that's like you. And it just hurts to see—to be in that position—knowing that there's nothing else out there but that f---ed up environment, you know?

But it was a struggle too, 'cause being raised in the projects, for a black dude, it's tough. It seems like you're an outsider from society. When we moved to different environments, I had a lot of fights when I was younger—school fights, gang fights, neighbourhood fights.

Also being in dysfunctional relationships with family members—my step dad giving me physical injuries—had a big impact on my life, very personal. My father wasn't in my life, so it kind of made an impact on me. I was around cats that was doing bad.

Like everyone else, my family deserved better opportunities. I thought it was that I didn't have no guidance, no choices in life. I was separated from society, you know—black person. It gave me that racist mentality, I guess, against white people, because I felt my family deserved an equal—no matter what—happier life. Not only that, I can't just say 'my peoples' in general, 'cause there's Latinos there, too… white people as well, but, a lot of Latinos and blacks in the hood. We haven't gotten along with each other. So I could never see myself chilling or hanging with somebody that wasn't in my situation. It was more like "Let me go hang out with this cat and that cat," and "Let's go out and let's join this." Feel me?

A LOVING MOTHER

My mom was the best a mom could ever be. She was a tough woman and she was strong. It was hard for her, welfare and five kids clothing, gifts for Christmas. Our fathers wasn't in our lives. My mother was struggling with us, things that most of my homies in the projects have in common.

I have four sisters and one brother now. But as I was growing up, being raised with four sisters was tough for me. I had to follow them, making sure they wasn't with n----s, you know? I was a big burden on my sisters, to my mother. I was like mama's boy, feel me? I grew up out of that, situation. I had to be strong, because we had no fatherly love or man, feel me?

One thing that I remember about my mom was that she taught me, she always said, "don't be a punk and a fool." 'cause it seems like every time I got into a fight, I got my ass whupped and the belt came out. So I always wondered why she said that and what she mean. Yeah, we got beatings and it was, hard times, but her love was everlasting. That's really what I'm trying to say. I believe that's the part of growing up that's good for learning lessons in life. But she always kept me in the books, kept me away from bad ass kids and all that. She always saw great aptitude in me and knew what my capacity and capability would bring in my life. Things like that.

This is the realization today: I realize that we must find ourselves by exploring our talents and character. I came to that realization the first time I got locked up for doing something bugged out. I was fourteen. I got arrested for something not really big and it changed my life. Somehow I ended behind bars again. Age fifteen, got caught smoking and ticketed without an ID. Sixteen, got caught hoping the subway turnstiles without and ID. Eighteen, got caught selling drugs—marijuana—to support my family. Nineteen, I'm fighting on the streets of Brooklyn. Twenty, being around the wrong people at the wrong time. And now, 23, present time… I've learned.

I KNOW WHO I AM AS A MAN:
FROM STRUGGLING BOY TO AN EASY MAN

From a young time in my life, I was destined to know who my father was. I felt that I needed to know my ancestral trail as a man—to who I was going to be later on in life. I had read somewhere before that a son that listens and is wise will make a mother proud, but a son that is blind makes a father ashamed. My father, the man I saw to be at the age of eight years old, from quick memory, was a guy with an enormous glow of ability in who he was. Strong minded, sociable, supporting and hardworking. My question for him is 'Why wasn't you there for me?' But I now know the truth, Dad. I thank you for being the honest and loving father that you are today. I've grown from a struggling boy to an easy growing man. Thanks to your fatherly advice and hard life that you've been through, changing for the better. So you can see my life right. I'll always love you and respect you as a loving father and a man of the Lord. As of today I know that mom is proud of me and you are as well. To know what true happiness and success is like one must walk through sorrow and struggle.

MY SCHOOL EXPERIENCE

I went to elementary school in Manhattan on the Lower East Side. I went to Junior High 135, Roberto Clemente 'til high school, JFK, Chelsea, Unity, EBC and to GED. Now I finally obtained my GED at the Horizon Academy.

I'd say my best school experience was from junior high school to high school. I didn't have a favorite grade. I was always an honor roll student, but I fell off in high school dropping out, to get high, cutting school. I joined in the wildin' out crowds from school.

My social studies teacher tried to pull me back and her name was Miss B. She was the meanest teacher in school, and I was accused of being a class clown, you know? I went from doing good, having good grades, to smoking bud. I was very smart, I got passed. One day, my parents had a parent-teacher conference and Miss B. told my mom, "He's a good student, but he's in a gang," and mom was shocked to hear that I was

gang-related. The principal let me go, for burning the school down, but she wanted me to stay 'cause she could see my potential.

It's funny, early in junior high school I had this appearance of glasses and curly hair and I looked like—what do you call it—a cornball, a nerd, a dweeb. But see, when I got into high school my whole M.O., my personality changed, feel me? The way I dressed changed. Like I had to leave that part of me where it was, at the time. We all reach a time where we want to change. It's not outside. It's inside. To me it felt like I had to change. So I had braids. I grew. I worked out to shape up—just to fit in. I started bagging shorties, rocking the latest name brands, and copping every cell phone. In high school, I completely changed.

I fell off, I guess. I guess I wanted to be down, or with it, and that's what I needed, popularity. Most of the young people want to be popular to everybody. In junior high school I had like nerdy, cornball friends. Then you meet a few cool guys you try to like, you know, balance the two groups. Soon it becomes impossible to balance; you've got to pick one or the other. Like a couple of days I hung out with my friends that's the cool guys, pulling me away, more and more away from my cornball friends. It's like that love, like you know, hanging out. I started to see from my feelings these guys is what I wanted to be with, and then it was time for me to go back to my sons. It was like, I was alone. I had to keep myself away from it all. It changed—high school's different. Like the fact I had friends—if I didn't have those cats I'd probably be lost, probably wouldn't known the social side. I had one Spanish, one Chinese friend and cats laughed at us, older tough guys, feel me? Yeah. And it didn't bother me at all at that point in life when I was like, "I need to just be cool and see what this is like." I lost my friends though, Franklin, Christopher and David. What's strange is that we didn't have tag names. A tag name is like my name is Mike but they call me Ferno, or Boy Slaughter. Folks with the most opportunities in the world is the ones with the tag names. Any name, like, you

Slaughter

know, like it could be Christopher, we call him D Lite, it's AKA, officially known as, feel me, this person and that person. Those were my good friends. Oh, we used to play basketball even though we didn't know how to play basketball for nothing.

IMPACT

There's different ways to be initiated. Certain gangs—it depends on color or the way of the gang—jumped in, or you gotta pop off to initiate yourself. Like for me, I was jumped in. I was jumped in the gang for about five minutes. So that's how it goes. They have the higher ranks, those who was the age I am now. I'm 22. We'd get together and we'd all have statuses. You obtained your status by doing things, like robbing people, innocent people on the street to prove your dedication to the gang. Like bringing someone home. See home is home of the gang, yeah. A set of the gang. That's the way that we get status up, like things you do. Drugs is one, you can't leave that out. There's a few older cats that's in the gang. They'll be the ones that have everything. So if you wanted to be down—they'll give us the heat and tell us to hold down—that's our protection.

I was fifteen when my mom knew what I was doing she was shocked. She'd be crying and she would hold my hand with this strong stare, you know? Those would be words I will never forget. She used to tell me, "None of these kids out here don't really care about you." Then she used to tell me about girls I used to buy things for. I was so in love with females for the wrong reasons, she used to tell me things, like, "You stop giving them everything. First find out if you love her. And you probably think sex is important, that's probably what it is." I didn't have to believe Mom, but she's always right. Mom is always right.

My step dad was abusive. Any little thing that I was caught doing, he was ready to put the fist on me. Box me up, you know? Give me a black eye. I look back at it and I say I'm glad he did that. It taught me about forgiving people and how to be a strong understanding man. My heart and my soul made me sensitive. Tough, though. I've been through hell. My step father… when I was younger he left marks on my body, like you know? I could take it. I wasn't soft. It made me a real man.

CHANGE

I'm tired of being tied up and being arrested. I'm 22 now, and I'm a father of one child. That's one important thing. I dropped my old ways because of my daughter. I changed and I surrendered to God. Not even, you know, this haven't made me, you know a spiritual person. I was always like that. I had to change, to the best of my ability. I became obsessed with reading anything and everything, lifestyles, locations, experiences and travelling more than usual to places I never been—to South Carolina, New Jersey, Pennsylvania, Albany, Rochester.

I would say that's one thing that black people that grow up in the projects don't know about, and that's religion. Our religion. All the spiritual tools—and who Jesus Christ, who

God is—and the impact they have on our life instead of just, you know, passing them out of our life. Not taking time to understand that we are living life with our Creator. If I had to mentor a young boy in the project I guess I could tell him, that there's love if he's

Slaughter

familiar, possibly familiar with love and if he would like to live a life of happiness and joy. Young kids today, get on to the rest of your life and know the difference between right and wrong.

BEING BROOKLYNIZED

Brooklyn was the roughest. It was more violent. Not that many options—not as many options in the Brooklyn projects as it is in Manhattan. I got into so many fights when I moved out there. My sisters used to get scared at times. I don't think about where I'm at. I got jumped a few times. When you get jumped, a group of pussies or cowards beat up an individual because they're all scared to have a one-on-one—because they are afraid to lose. Oh man, every time this happened it made me feel like I didn't know who to

blame, feel me? I couldn't blame my mom. None of us could blame my mom. It was just, you know, we hated the fact that we used to always worry, you know? Sad at the fact of being in Brooklyn. Then there was times where I'd lay down, try not to see it.

WRONG FATHERLY LOVE

I was like a kid with the most problems, always got into something. I had experience with abuse. My father was in my life until I was like nine years old. But he started popping in my life here and there, being the best dad a boy can dream to have. My stepfather would leave bruises on me by boxing me up all the time. My mom, she didn't do anything. What could she do? Last time I saw him years ago, he came over to Brooklyn to our front door. The first thing I thought about was killing him. I opened the front door and had a knife with me, too. I pulled my shirt back over and listened to what he had to say. This man had the nerve to cry. He had the nerve. He ain't nothing to me. But he acted all humble and said that he was sorry and he loved me. Yeah. I don't know what to say, you know? He had the Koran with him. I'm grown now. It wasn't the same scene. I had a choice, I could be the big man, you know? I could turn my life around and forgive him. I closed the door and he was standing outside, still waiting. He waited for three long hours and he waited and rang the bell again 'cause he was in tears. I still had rage and I had revenge my heart. I decided to let him in. So I did. He came in, put his bag down by the closet door, folded his hands as if changed and apologized for everything. He admitted everything that he did, and we accepted it.

That was the first time that my younger sisters had seen their father. Mom had two sets of twins, me and my sister, and a younger set of twins. They're teenagers now. So I'll say this is about maybe three years ago. The first time they see their pops after awhile and knew who he was, he finally explained himself and my mom forgave him.

Later we learned to love him. So again, I put that behind me. I still had the knife behind me. Something in me changed that day. That was the main, I think, that was the main purpose. To make a first life choice that would benefit me for future reference. 'cause I saw only pain in my life. I looked for kids with the same problem, you know, growing up in the area where society is like that. But it was hard on my mother, you know, raising a family on her own. I'm glad to be the person who I am today.

Slaughter

LIFE'S CONCLUSION

We must overcome our worldly problems. We're all spiritual beings who are mutually dependent upon one another. Our lives are more important and filled with meaning. Because when we all die some day, only then will we face death and find out death has no favor to sinners. Choose to have life after death for eternity or choose death for your second life in total darkness or Hell. To waste your life's time by being ignorant with knowledge is an insult and disgrace to your soul. We must make a change in learning and obeying the three laws of existence- which are the physical, universal and spiritual laws, by educating ourselves to become a united family of different colours living in peace and harmony. But is that possible within these walls?

Mi Vida Loca

SOSA

WHAT I CAN REMEMBER: MY LIFE IN MEXICO

Growing up was pretty hard. I came to the U.S. when I was seven years old. I came from Mexico at the age of seven, started going to school here in the Bronx, at PS 95. It was pretty hard because I didn't know the language; I didn't know how to write the language. It took me about three months to learn English and then start speaking it.

But coming to the country wasn't hard like for other people. Because my mother, although she's pure Mexican, her skin color is pretty much white. So what we did is we passed right over the bridge from Mexico to the U.S. Immigration stopped her and asked her for ID, but when she was looking for it and she pulled out American dollars, they believed that she was from the U.S., with her skin color. And they just let me and my brother and my mother pass, and we just came right into the U.S. That was 1992.

I really don't remember how we got to the border from Mexico City. But we went to Tijuana and then crossed over and went to Texas. Then we took a plane straight here, to New York, and I've been here ever since.

I remember little parts about Mexico City. I remember when I was five or six, we used to be broke, so broke that to get to school instead of like taking a bus—over there in Mexico you get on the trucks—there's things you can grab on behind it where you just jump on top and take it to school.

Over there the teachers have more power. They could actually hit you if you don't do what you're supposed to do. So you know, they get more respect than teachers over here. I learned a little bit in school in Mexico City, but not that much that I can remember it today. I can't really remember learning much from my family while was there either. Not really. I just remember that the school was about like six, seven blocks from where I used to live. That's about it.

Sosa

ALWAYS TOGETHER: MY BRONX STORY

I remember coming here, to school in the Bronx, and the first day of school. It was hard. I got treated differently because everybody saw me, you know, I came dressed different than them. I was wearing, like regular clothes, and as soon as I came to school everybody was wearing name brand stuff. They started picking on me, "Oh, you ain't got money. You're broke," this and that. They just treated me different. I couldn't speak the language. I started looking for Spanish kids to talk to.

It was hard, too. People used to pick on me 'til I was about seventh – no, like fifth, sixth grade, because my mother always told me, "Don't start problems." But she said, "once somebody puts a hand on you, it doesn't matter, but don't let nobody pick on you." Then after that I was just… forget it. I ain't gonna take anything from nobody.

So people still tried picking on me until they saw me start to just stand up for myself. One time, my brother, my little brother, who is now twenty years old, he was in—well, he was in third grade, I was in fourth grade. For some lucky reason, the teacher that I had that year, next year my brother would have that teacher. That teacher was pretty good with us. There was a student in this class that kept on picking on my brother 'cause this other kid was bigger. So my brother would come to me and say, "Oh look, this guy is picking on me and I don't know what to do. He has a lot of friends." After school, the bus would leave us right across the street from a park. That guy was waiting for my brother that day at that bus stop where we got off the yellow school bus and he tried to kick my brother and we ended up hitting him. And then his friends came hitting us. As soon as they saw that we were defending ourselves they backed up. They thought that we were going to stay and let ourselves be hit. They were going to jump us, but we both just started swinging at them.

And then after that they would try it, but there was two of us, they couldn't do that much. We'll take a hit or two, but we're going to hit back. So after that, me and my brother were like this, we were always together. We learned a lot of stuff together. 'Til about last year, yeah.

THINGS CHANGED: THE MOVE TO BROOKLYN

I pretty much done everything real good in school 'til I got to high school, like a lot of other people. Things changed. I lived in the Bronx for about three or four years. Then I moved to Brooklyn to the neighborhood of Williamsburg. It was back in 1997. I became gang-related. My brother became gang-related a year after me. So everything I did—we pretty much followed each other, from going out to parties, getting girls, getting into fights, getting into trouble. Cutting school, they always seemed to catch me my brother together, we were always cutting school. It's pretty much the same thing. I was the older brother, but there was very high—I don't know, like a respect between my brother and I. Like I know what he is, what he's capable of. And he's the same towards me.

Williamsburg was better because it was a Spanish neighborhood, so I got along more better. That was when I was in seventh grade, and I started messing around, me and

my brother. We went to IS 49 on Graham Avenue, and we were there for a couple of years. And then we moved to Manhattan, to 36th Street. And I think that's a pretty good neighborhood. I still went to school in Brooklyn, so I'd take the subway in the morning to get to school.

Sosa

After the move, people stopped messing with us. Because people here, they don't know me or my brother or how we act or how we are towards people. Then it depended on, like, how you carry yourself, how you talk to people and know that you show respect to somebody—you're expecting to get it back. So that's pretty much about it. We started speaking to other people, and like I was saying, it was a Spanish neighborhood, so everybody pretty much got more along. I mean I had just pretty much less problems. There was instances where people tried to do it, but not as before. They tried to pick on me, or my brother. Then we did the same thing, we ended up fighting, and they stopped. When we moved I didn't like it because we had been already for some time in the Bronx. But after we were there we enjoyed it. And then, now Bushwick is even better.

EVEN BETTER: MOVING TO BUSHWICK

Bushwick is my neighborhood. I've been there for about four or five years already. Everybody knows each other, everybody grew up in that neighborhood, grew up with each other pretty much. So I moved in about '99, around that time. So—no, it was about 2000, 2001. And we grew up with people around the block, like growing up over there. So we had a lot of friends.

So pretty much now we know everybody. Nobody has problems with us. We're always hanging out. It's just a lot better. The only thing is, it's a bad neighborhood, but people don't mess with you unless they don't know you. If they know you they know who you are and they don't mess with you. There's a lot of drugs, a lot of drugs. You hear shootings around there sometimes. Cops over there stopping people for no reason.

And as we moved I had to learn to carry myself. Who taught me? Nobody. Me. I had to learn it by myself because I never had a father to tell me this or that. My mother was always there, but she was always working, so I'm getting into problems with other people because I'm the type of person that, I don't have no hair on my tongue. If I have to say something to you, I'm going to say it. Even if it gets me in problems. But I'm going to say it. I can't hold something in.

My brother's a different person. He's the quiet-type person. He'll hold something in to a certain point and then he'll just blow up on somebody. I just won't take it. And, from getting into that I learned like how people, how to talk to somebody. Like before, I never used to go off on somebody; show them respect. But I don't play around with people—like other people play fight a lot—'cause I know somebody's going to end up hurt. And like I try to do that here. I don't like people playing around me or playing with me because I know, 'cause I'm in a place like this, playing around might carry itself to a real argument, or a real problem.

When I was in IS 49—when I got into a fight with somebody else—like after they see that you stand up for yourself and that you're not going to let somebody push you down like they're better than you and, you know? So I got into a fight with a dude because of some stupid, I don't even remember what we got into a fight about, but everybody saw that we don't let nobody push us around, so they respect us for that.

I don't remember this dude's name. He was a big, dark-skinned guy. Big guy. I was like ten. He was about a year-and-a-half older, two years older than me. He was a big guy compared to my size. But since my mother told me, "If somebody touches you, hit them back. It doesn't matter. I'll go to school. It doesn't matter if they call me, say 'Your son got into a fight.'" Then we just stopped caring because, okay, our mother's going to come. That would, that—how do you call it? I wasn't scared like before with the feeling to hit somebody for trying to touch us or pick on us. As you lose that, that thought of being scared, of fighting back, it just changes everything.

It was like my mother, when my mother said this, it was like turning on a switch in my head. The first time she told me this, it was back when I was like in fourth or fifth grade, but we were never fighting as much with other people 'til we got to Williamsburg. They started picking on us a little bit and she told us, "Oh, you guys don't listen. You can fight back. I won't get into a problem with, argue with you, or let's say reprimand for standing up for yourself. If you're standing up for yourself, it's good. But just don't go start off problems for no reason."

Yeah, pretty much turned the switch when somebody tried to pick on me. Let them talk and talk and talk to a certain extent, because words can hurt you. Once they start crossing that line then that's a lot of—either you're going to shut up or I'm going to make you shut up. Because people like those ears, like talking loud about peoples' families, they want to talk s___. It doesn't matter, and I don't take it, especially around my mother, 'cause my mother's been my father and mother.

I learned everything from my mother. I mean, she does jewelry, so she makes it, she does soldering, like for earrings and stuff. We used to have a company that makes jewelry in Manhattan, 36th Street. We used to make the jewelry. From when I was little I had—I don't know, I used to help out. I don't like—I like to keep busy. So we used to, I used to know how to make, I still know how to make casting and cleaning and polishing. I know how to do gold. I know how to do gold, silver, precious metal, all pretty much cleaning, polishing, making it.

So I know a lot of the people from 42nd Street down that does jewelry. I know everybody 'cause I pretty much grew up there doing that.

My mom still does it, and she tells me, "Well why don't you get your education?" 'Cause me, I've been working a lot for the past couple of years, I've been just pretty much work in restaurants. And where I started working from busboy and then moving up to runner and then moving up to waiter. So I pretty much moved up to being a manager in an Italian restaurant in Brooklyn. She's telling me before, "Like look, look what you make in a day or you make in a week. Well you do the whole week, I work for maybe a day and I make that much money."

She said that about herself because she made that much money making jewelry. What I made in a week she makes in a day. So she be like, "Go to school. I'm not asking you to help me around the house. I'm not asking you to work for nothing. You don't need to work. I just want you to go to school."

BUT I DON'T KNOW: HIGH SCHOOL LIFE

But I don't know, once you're in school and you get to high school, it's like change. You've got to pay for cutting school, not like when you were in junior high school, or nothing. Going to parties—I went to hooky parties, or just pretty much hanging out. You could, like I went to a school where they'd let you out for lunch. And me, I would go outside, go to the park, but I won't come back. I'll just stay outside hanging out. That's what started messing me up. I was doing pretty good. I was taking computer programming. I just got off track when I left high school.

I remember the first time I cut class. It was a whole bunch of girls that I knew when I used to go to Grady High School that were like, "Oh, come on, we've got a hooky party all the way over in Sunset Park. Come with us. We're going to go hang out, we're going to drink, we're going to relax, chill out." And I was like, "No, what if they catch us? You know, I don't want to get in trouble."

So we keep on talking about it and talking about it for days before, and then the day came and I was like, "F--- it. What's the worst that could happen? I get caught cutting school and what, they'll just call my house and I'll get in trouble. But it better be worth it."

So we went to the party, we ended up drinking. After we ended up drinking, relaxing, and dancing. From early in the morning 'til like 3:00 in the afternoon when school finished, a party. And then we went back to school the next day like nothing, going back to class. I noticed that the teachers didn't ask no questions, they didn't ask me, "Why you didn't come to school?" I was like, "Okay, you can do this."

Oh yeah, it was worth it. 'Cause there was a whole lot of girls. A couple of them started dancing and we got drunk. Actually it was fun.

High school was the best. I still miss high school. I wish I could go back. I don't know, I like being around people. I like being around school.

When I came here, to my knowledge I didn't have a GED 'cause I took the GED test a year and a half ago in Edward Murrow High School. I gave my address from when I lived in Flatbush. This is my home address. But the mailing address where they were supposed to send my results and my diploma was my mother's address, which we've been in Bushwick for five or six years. But I never received my scores or my diploma, so I thought that I didn't pass it. So then I've been in school here for about a month, a month or so. And come to tell me, they called me yesterday out of class, and they tell me, "I should kick your ass because you took your GED and you're just taking the classes here for what?" I was like, "What do you mean I passed my GED?" He's like, "Yeah, you took the test before and you passed it." Okay, yeah, but to my knowledge if I would've passed the test, I would've had my diploma.

But they, they're telling me that I have to pay to get a copy of my diploma. I don't want a copy. I want my diploma, 'cause they made a mistake, they didn't send me my diploma. If not, I would not have taken the classes again.

At the same time, the diploma means a better life for me here. And in Mexico, if I go back. Because over there a lot of people don't get to go to school. They finish like high school, junior high school here and some people just stop going to school and start working.

READING PEOPLE: LIFE IN THE RESTAURANT BUSINESS

I tried to get a job in the restaurant business 'cause I like talking. That's how I make more money. I make more money in the restaurant as a waiter talking to people, you know? I learned this wherever I was at, going to different restaurants, they'd tell me it's not what the person wants to buy when they come in the restaurant, it's what you want to sell them. It's more psychological—you talk to them and you see what they like. "Okay, you know what, I think you're going to like this," and most of the time I get people to buy whatever I want.

I learned this over the years, and it worked real good until I got arrested and I came here. I was the waiter and then they moved me up to manager. I was already taking care of schedules and money and ordering wine and beer and all that. After working in ten, fifteen restaurants, I had learned how to read people.

It was Valentine's Day last year, this year. So we had—see, in the restaurant we took, 'cause usually in the restaurant where I was at we don't take reservations. First come, first served. It used to get full. We got people calling from like a month a month-and-a-half before, "Yeah, I want to make reservations for Valentine's."

So they had a couple of desserts, special desserts, and some of that and like we used to have a plate… lobster with homemade black fettuccini. So of course, for each plate we charged about forty dollars. And we would push that. My boss would be like, "Okay, now we've got, we have like twelve, thirteen orders of this." So the different waiters I'm working with, there used to be only two of us, just me and another guy, I'm like, "Okay, we got this much left for tonight, you know? Sell like eight of these, for a special, and you take this, you sell this." So the whole night we'll push that.

There was a guy on Valentine's Day from the UN came, they took a whole big table, like 15 guys, and I sold the same thing to like about six of them. Starting from the specials, from special soup to special desserts, main course, special salad. That day I made money. I made, in one day I made like about six hundred dollars in tips.

I just love it. And I, 'cause I like dressing up. I don't like dressing like this—like I am now. I like dressing up. I got my tailored suits and all this. I just love it. Within the restaurant they dress casual, but to me, I mean, if we're charging you forty dollars for plate of food, you're expecting something. You're not expecting to come dressed in a t-shirt and pants. I'm expecting you to be nicely dressed, you know.

Although my boss didn't like it, I came in dressed up every day. And then he got to the point where he would just—before he used to tell me, "You've got to start dressing more casually." I'd be like, "I don't like it." I used to argue with him about that, "If we're going to charge them so much for a plate, they're expecting more of us." Yeah, I know it's a family restaurant and you just gotta get used to me just dressing up.

People started asking for me when I used to come, like I used to have my own customers already that would come every week. I'll give them a bottle of wine on the house and they wouldn't even get mad about it, you know, because they know in the long run they're just already customers. Like I had a guy that owned a travel agency, which he was going to give us tickets to go to Tahiti for my boss, just on him, because how we used to treat him when he came in. He didn't have to wait for no table 'cause, "Oh, yeah, I got you." I would put him at the front of the line. Usually there used to be a line to come into the restaurant. You know, I'd put him all the way in the front, give him a table.

You make a lot of connections in a restaurant. I met guys from the music industry. Marc Anthony once ate over there. A couple of Yankees ate over there. It was great. I started seeing like people, actors coming in to eat, and then other people'd be like, "Damn, I would love to…" People get crazy when they see an actor, but after you start seeing them often—like we had a guy that used to work in that soap opera that used to come to the restaurant every day. And you start seeing, he comes with his hat on and like dressed on him, he'll come in every week and then finally somebody started noticing, "Oh my god." And for a good while and I used to know what his kids ordered, you know, I take care of him, and he take care of me. He be like, "Oh, if you want to come to the show when they're taping it one of these days, just tell me. I'll get you in." Oh man, I mean, you get a lot of connections. I met a lot of people.

And so when I wanted to go back to school then I was already starting to save up money to go back to school for computers, but then I got arrested and that was pretty much it. Over some b---s---.

MORE DREAMS: COMPUTERS

I started learning about computers in high school where I was doing programming.

Computers changed everything. I mean, before there was no Internet, there was only the phone. There was nothing. You know? Computers changing everything. Computers are the future.

From when I started going to school in the Bronx and we used to be always—they used to always give us classes and typing and Kid Pics and all that, drawing and doing whatever. I started typing and then people started saying, "Oh man, you can type fast. Why don't you type this for me? I'll give you something." I thought to myself I can make something out of this.

Then I started messing with pictures, cutting peoples' heads off and putting other peoples' faces in the pictures. Yeah, they're fun but, I don't know, it just attracted me from when I was little. And the other thing that attracted me was pretty much sound systems. But then I started—after a while that I got to know computers I started knowing how to get the programs, so I don't have to borrow the equipment for DJ, you just download the program and buy the equipment. I don't have to buy a thousand CDs and have cases, you just have it on one hard drive.

And then I just started doing a lot. Lately I just bought me a Vaio, one of the new Vaios that came out, and then now for no reason I didn't get to use it. I was just practicing more on the DJ coming, because I know a lot of people in music that DJ. So I got a DJ program and I was showing them how to use it. And some people around the neighborhood that don't know how to use a computer, I was about to start giving them classes, start charging them.

AND AFTER ALL THIS ...

I don't know, like the case that I have now, they're telling me about I might get deported to Mexico because I still don't have my paperwork straight. That makes me feel like, "Damn, and I've been there this whole time," I know that I'm not going to get used to the change as quick in Mexico. Over there you work there so much for so little money. I'm already used to making money here.

My brother got deported. He got, he was making so much here, and he was making about what, ten dollars, ten or eleven dollars a day over there? I know we're not used to that. We're used to making money here. So it's a real change.

I haven't spoken to my brother since I've been here, a few months. But before? Oh, every day, every week! I'd talk to him every two or three days. 'Cause now he's building a—we bought land in Mexico because my mother is getting older, so we don't want her to work no more. So she wants to go back to Mexico. We bought land in Veracruz. It's right by the ocean. We bought land over there. And my brother, since he got deported last year, right now we don't want him to work for himself 'cause we send him money from here. But he bought the land and he's already building our house over there for my mother. Soon she's going to want to go back. It's tough. We did so much here—and no we'll lose everything, pretty much. Because we put in an application for paperwork in 2001 and still didn't get no answer, or nothing. We keep on paying the lawyer like for no reason.

Yeah, sometimes I don't know, because I've seen other people that applied like last year, year-and-a-half ago, and they get an answer from Immigration so quick. And I'm like, "What's the difference?" I mean I've been here pretty much my whole life. I don't remember anything about Mexico that I can relate to. I'm a New Yorker; I grew up here. The only thing is that I was born over there.

And people take things for granted over here. I can't own a car. I could own a car, but I can't get caught driving it 'cause then I'll get arrested for driving with no license. I could buy a house, but what good does it do if I get deported? There's other things that I can't do that I wish I could. I can't go to college, or I can't get legal aid help like other people do to go to college. If I go to college, first I gotta work however many years to save up the money to go to college, or take it slow. I can't do any of that. I can't even go into the Armed Forces. I don't know, it's crazy.

I've pretty much grown up, and we couldn't do a lot of stuff that other people could. When I wanted to get me a cell phone. Okay, I can't get a cell phone on a plan with minutes because I don't have no credit, and I have no credit because I don't have a social security number, even though I've been here so long. I can't even put it in my mother's name because she doesn't have one either. I mean, we waste so much money on prepaid calling plans on a cell phone because I can't get a plan.

My friend was giving me a car. He was giving me a Mustang. From North Carolina he came over here. He was going to give me a Mustang but I wanted to tell him, "I can't have it." I could drive, sure, I could drive like nothing. I love driving. But I can't get caught in the city driving because after 9/11 you have checkpoints all over the place. I'm going to get stopped and get arrested, end up doing some time in here for nothing. Even now, you get arrested for no ID, you're going into jail.

Then you got people that, I mean, they say that immigrants here in the U.S., we're taking up just space and resources. But they don't understand that the U.S. was built on immigration. Nobody in the U.S. is an actual American unless they're Indians, as you say. We make everything go round, pretty much around the U.S. And I get mad when people talk about, "Oh, you're an immigrant. Go back to your country, man." You better learn that if we wasn't here, you think things are expensive now? Try sending somebody that went to college to go pick the cotton, cut the fruits and stuff. It makes me just mad.

Even in this class, and next door, I mean everywhere, there are heated discussions because the English teacher'd be like, "Okay, write an essay on something that is working now and had an impact on your life." I wrote about why Congress should pass a Dream Act, which they did for people like me that got, right now I've got my GED. That we would be able to get the chance to go to college or join the Armed Forces, which would then open up doors for me to become a citizen. And then I was like why would that affect me? Because I pretty much grew up here, I went to school here, and did everything. What would be the point of their trying to deport the immigrants here when a lot of them don't know any different? And you have people in the class who be like, "Oh, it doesn't matter; you're still an immigrant, this and that." I was like, "Where you from? What country you from?" "I'm American. I was born here." Okay, but this happens to one of your family members, they were an immigrant at one point, right?

Just because you were born here, because of that I was like, "What happens to me if I get deported? I still have a son here. What, are they going to keep my son over here?" I don't know, I guess, I read, I mean I read the newspaper every day. I read a lot. I have time. I read the paper, and I keep on reading about how—in a good way, when Governor Spitzer came into power, he said that he was going to try to do what he said with the drivers license for illegal immigrants because he knows how the city moves around, how much people work here that actually do help and not doing crime, they came here to work. He was going to give the license and so, so it was a step forward. So I was looking forward to it because if I was to get out of this, with me getting my drivers license over here, it would've opened up a whole bunch of doors.

I would've probably been able to get my car. Even I could've gotten a car and started working, driving a cab. They make money. Not like other people, that opens just a whole bunch of doors just for the drivers' license. Just to get our position and they get to turn it down and he turns back anyway. It was supposed to be now in December that he was supposed to do it.

A LIFE CHANGING EXPERIENCE: MY SON

My son was born June 24, 2004. I was eighteen. It just changed my life. I used to be wild. And when my son was born it just changed my life. I was working; I wasn't hanging out no more. It pretty much changed my life. I was pretty much working, going to school. Going to work, coming back home. It was the great—it's the best feeling in the world to have a son to come home to. Oh man. I used to come home after working the restaurant at 11:00. Not even, some 11:00, sometimes when I get out early. And as soon as my son would hear the door, he'd even be sleeping, I don't know how he knew, he would get up, he'll run to the door and with his arms out, "Daddy!" It was the best thing in the world.

Then my wife was older. I was with her when I was seventeen and she was 24. So we had a relationship. She's older than me. She was 24. Now she's 30 and I'm 22 and when I moved with her we moved out of my house by ourselves. I don't know, people started telling her, because she met other people and they started telling her, "Oh listen, he might be cheating" and this and that, "because he's younger. He goes out. He stays out all day." And I'm like, "I'm at work. What do you expect?" Because when I got the job as managing the restaurant it's

not like I could take many days off, I had to be there. If somebody doesn't show up to work I have to cover. It's my responsibility now. I took the job for a reason.

So then some people won't come into work and I have to show up. I have to leave what I'm doing, whatever it is, and go to work. She would think I was just using work as an excuse and I would get mad. So we started having problems because of it, 'cause this lady from under, that lived one floor under us, was telling her, "Oh, he's younger than you. He's cheating on you. He's…" I ended up having problems. She left to Florida, where her family lives, in December. Like two days before Christmas of last year she left to Florida with her family. Didn't even say nothing. I came back from work and my house was empty, didn't find my kid, didn't find my wife. That's what pretty much f---ed my life up, from that point on.

We have four rooms, a big place in Flatbush. I got a big apartment because I had my son with her, but she had—she still had some kids from her previous relationship and her kids grew up with me, so I saw them as my own. They're my kids, even though her oldest daughter is 13. She called me Daddy from when she was like six. She grew up with me. She didn't have no problems with that. Her other son is seven, going eight now. And we had four rooms, so the kids would have one room, we'd have one room, and we had an extra room. So I started renting the room to somebody that I knew and they were gone, you know. I knew he was good, he used to work and do what he did, come home.

So he came home that day, I opened the door and usually when I came in the door I hear my son. No, he's—I'm expecting him to come to the door and run at me, "Daddy," you know. And I don't see nobody. I walk in, none of my stuff is there, all of my DJ equipment, she had given away. And my friend was like, "Yo, what the hell happened?" I was like, I didn't know, you know?

I didn't know that she had gone to Florida 'til about a month later. The lady from downstairs that kept on telling her s---, luckily for me I know somebody that lives next to her, 'cause as soon as that happened I moved out of there. I couldn't live there. So they told me that he heard from her that she had gone to Florida, which is where I believe that she's at now.

And I haven't been able to contact her or my son in almost a year, which has messed me up.

So I started going out and I got drunk and I started smoking weed more heavily to try to relax my nerves. 'Cause I start thinking, "Where's my son? Is he good? Is he eating good?" I don't know. She took about ten thousand dollars that I had saved up that should've lasted, you know, for some time. But money runs out and I don't know how far her family's going to help her with it, so. It just keeps me just thinking.

I kind of wonder what's with him today. He's going to be four, just turned three in June.

FUTURE

Because I speak to my lawyer and he tells me, "Okay, they might get you with five years probation, but then you have to go to Immigration and fight your case, see if they'll let you stay in the country." And if, say if I got deported, then I can't come back into the country legally for five to ten years. And I know for a fact I'm not going to—I'm going to be in Mexico maybe for three-four months tops, and then I'm turning right back around and coming this way. I might end up doing time for it, but I'm not going to be over there thinking "What's in my son? What's he doing? Is he good?"

My mother tells me, "If you get deported back to Mexico I don't want you coming back." She says, "It's just going to bring you more problems. You might get arrested again over some b---s---- and do time." To me, right now, it doesn't matter. I just have to find out where to find my son and try to move forward in life. I mean, in here I'm in school trying to do something better for me, but...

Detras De Estas Paredes	*Behind These Walls*
Detras de estas paredes	*Behind these Walls*
Yo no peudo aser nada	*I can't do nothing,*
Detras de estas paredes	*Behind these walls,*
La gente dise ser muy mala	*People say they're really bad*
Detras de estas paredes	*Behind these walls,*
Yo no puedo caminar	*I can't even walk*
Ni hablar con mi hijo	*Or talk to my son*
Que me ase asta llorar	*That sometimes makes me cry*
Detras de estas paredes	*Behind these walls,*
Yo me tengo que aguantar	*I have to hold on*
El dolor que le causo a mi madre	*To the pain that I cause to my mother*
Del que no puedo hablar	*The one that can't be spoken of*
Detras de estas paredes	*Behind these walls,*
Yo no tengo mi familia	*I don't have my family,*
Lo que tengo es unos tipos	*What I have is a couple of guys*
Que son como mi familia	*That act like they my family*
Detras de estas paredes	*Behind these walls,*
Yo me tengo que quedar	*I have to stay,*
Hasta que un juez decida mi vida	*'Til a judge decides my life,*
Si me tengo que quedar.	*Maybe I have to stay.*

Sosa

Ups and Downs

Magic

GROWING UP

Well, growing up, you know, when I was younger, I pretty much had it... pretty much had it all, really. I lived in Long Island with my parents—I never met my real dad, but I lived with my stepfather—my mom was with my stepfather. While I lived there, I used to get in trouble a lot in school.

When I was, like, fourteen, I ended up in a juvenile detention center and I ended up going to an evaluation center—Saint Mary's Group Home—for two months. They were going to send me upstate to a longer facility, Lincoln Hall, to keep working on my behavior and all that, but my mom, she told them that she wants me back. She wanted me back home. And she took me out.

I went to Bossi School in Long Island and I used to get in trouble there all the time. I ended up in one of... a mental health-like school, like, to help 'cause I was diagnosed with bipolar and ADHD. They sent me to this other school, Woodward, at Freeport, Long Island, and I was there for like a couple of years. But, the second year that I was there, I had gotten into an incident with my stepfather at home and I had hit him, 'cause he hit me. He used to hit me. He used to hit me since I was little. So, I was old enough now and everything. I felt when he hit me right there, I was about fifteen, I started hitting him back and it got into a big fight. After that, he called the cops, and I got kicked out of the house. So then I moved out to where I am now in Queens. Woodside, Queens.

KICKED OUT

Yeah, I was about fifteen. I was at my girlfriend's house and I had school the next day. I had come home late... I came in pretty late. My mom and my parents were still up. When I came in, I snuck in through the window, so he got mad. He heard me and he seen me and he

Magic

was a little… he was drinking a little bit. And I had came home with a friend, too.

So, when I climbed through the window, I went to open the door for a friend, and he was like, "Oh, what are you doing?" He was screaming and I'm like, "Oh, listen, I'm just going to get something, I'm going to leave, right? I'm going to leave real quick. I don't even want to see you," 'cause we had gotten into an argument the day before. I was like, "I just want to get something for my friend that I need to give him and he's going to leave right now. I'm going to leave, too."

And he called—my friend was black—he was like, "Take that n----- out of my house." And that offended me, because that put me in a position, you know, that put my friend in a position and it put me in a position to feel, you know, offended because that's my friend. You know, I bring him to my house and I don't… he doesn't deserve to be called that, you know, treated that way.

So after that, I'm like… I start yelling at him, but I really kind of blacked out. I don't remember what I said, really. And he goes and slaps me in the face. Once he slaps me, my instant reaction was I hit him. I gave him a left hook and he was surprised, he held his face. Once he held his face, I rushed him. I threw him to the corner and I kept hitting him. My mom and my little sister came out, they got in between. I didn't want to keep attacking him because they woulda got hurt.

So I was yelling and I tried to keep going around my mother and my sister to hit him again. And my friend comes and says, "Ritchie, Ritchie, what are you doing? What are you doing?" And he pulls me out from the middle of my mom and my stepdad and my sister. He pulls me, like, "What are you doing?" He drags me all the way to the outside and he gives me a place to stay that night.

The next morning I tried to go back home. I knock on my mother's windows—I know my dad had already left for work in the morning. So, I knock on my mother's windows because they lock the doors on the house and I didn't have no keys, and she said, "You know, Ritchie, just go to your grandma's. Don't come back, 'cause he doesn't want you here no more." Dah dah dah, you know. I was like, "You know what? Whatever."

The next day, I hung out at my friend's house until night came and I ended up having nowhere to stay, so I slept on my porch roof until the morning and knocked on my window again. Then I went to my grandma's house in Queens, and ever since then, I stayed there. But the incident with my father... after the years, like now we're, we're... you know, we're not in bad blood anymore. But there was a couple of years, like four years, before we started talking again.

HE STILL CARES

I was nineteen when I started talking to him again. I was going through some real—I was having an episode, a bipolar episode, and I ended up in a mental hospital in a psych ward. My mom was telling me all, "Look, your stepdad really wants to see you. He's concerned with you." She was going on. And then, you know, I started wondering, you know, he even wants to see me... he still cares, you know, whatever. So one day I let him in. He came to the mental hospital and we started talking again.

Four years. I didn't even see him. I didn't even know—I think I never went, like, inside my house for the next four years. Like, my parents house, I wasn't even in front of it, I was just... I stayed in Queens for the next four years. I used to go back to Long Island and visit my friends mostly, but I never went to the house and I didn't see my mom for like a year. But then, she started coming to my grandma's house a lot.

So after that, you know, everything got good. After three weeks, I got out of the

Magic

psych wards and, yeah, I saw him. It was weird. I was like, "Oh man." I was like, "This feels awkward." I gave him a hug and everything. I was like, "Oh, how you doing?" He was like, "I love you." So now I was like… I felt awkward, like I didn't know what to say. We never brought that back up. Yeah. We left that a dead issue.

I WENT BACK HOME

After three weeks, when I got out finally, I went back home. I went back to my house. It's a nice little house in Long Island, and I went back there and then it was totally different. It was really nice. I don't know, it was like, you know, they upgraded the inside, and a little bit of the outside. They had added some things to the house, like this driveway, another driveway. They had a fence in the backyard. It was really nice, and it's just… I wasn't used to it, so I had the imagination of the old house. That kind of made me feel bad, you know? Because it was like, as soon as I leave, you know, they upgrade everything! They have everything all nice, you know? Like, you know, it's better off that I stay out of their life, you know, 'cause they look like they're living way better like that, you know? So after that, I just… ever since, I've been talking to him, you know? And this had happened just last year, around this time. Ever since, we've been talking, you know, same old same old.

I STILL SEE HIM AS A FATHER

I still see him as a father. He's been there since I was, like, two years old. He raised me… he's done a lot of things for me. He bought me—he used to buy me a lot of video games. He used to buy me, you know, a lot of things. He used to spoil me, too. He spoiled my sister more, 'cause it's his real daughter, you know, it's his daughter daughter. I'm not his real son. But he used to spoil me, too. You know, he used to give me what I wanted.

But I used to remember him, he used to—I just remember he used to always take me to work and give me like ninety dollars a day and I was, like, only fourteen. He owns his own little gardening company—construction company and all that. He does construction, paints. He does a lot of things… carpenter and all that. He'd give me like 90 dollars every time I went, but I never really worked—I used to spend it on toys. My friends, me and my friends used to go eat. I'd spend it on, you know, video games. When I was thirteen, I was still into toys. I was buying all these Spawn action figures and all this—Marvel, you know, superhero figures. I was just… I'd go buy videogames, go to the mall, took my friends with me. You know, have a good time with the money. But, when I was fourteen… when I already turned like fourteen, fifteen, I was getting a little loose. It was kind of my, you know… I was growing up or whatever, and I had a girlfriend. I always used to come home late. I always used to hang out late, you know? I used to be disrespectful. I never used to listen to him, 'cause he was always a strict, strict person.

And I don't know, ever since I've been like fourteen, fifteen, I never, I mean I never really, really, really got along with him. We always had a problem, 'cause he was always so strict, but it never got to the point when I was like, fifteen or something, when I got into that level in terms of violence and all that, 'cause he was trying to better me and discipline me. You know, he was trying to help me out. He wasn't—you know, I just looked at it the wrong way, you know? Now that I'm older… Back then, I seen it like, "Oh no, he just wants to bother me. He just wants somebody to bother, 'cause he doesn't want to…" You know? Like, "He doesn't say nothing to my little sister, you know, he always says something to me. I'm always the one getting in trouble." Well, it's true, see, I'm always the one that was doing bad things, you know.

I'M ALWAYS THE ONE GETTING IN TROUBLE

This one time, my mother's plants... me and my little sister were both playing there and we were playing with a ball. She had these big plants, I don't know, in the house. You know, huge plants in pots and all that. And we were playing with a ball and all that and I threw it to my sister real hard and she didn't catch it and it hits the plant. The plant pot tips over and all the dirt's on the floor and all of that. And I'm like, telling my sister, "Oh man," I'm like... my mom comes out and my stepfather comes out. The first thing he does is come and grabs me. He's like, "What the hell you doing?" You know, he gives me these little... he hits me, like, in the head a little bit, and he kicks me right in my, you know, kicks my behind and all that.

So he sends me into my room. I come back down and I'm screaming at him, "How do you know she didn't do it?" I was there for like five seconds. I went up to my room, I came back down and I was crying and I was like, "Why do you always attack me? You never tell her. You never tell my sister anything. You know, you always assume it's my fault, dah dah dah." And he was like, he didn't pay attention. He didn't pay no mind to me, and that's what got me even more mad. He was cleaning the mess up! I was angry and I ran upstairs and I was like "Arrgh!" and I kicked my door real hard and when I kicked real hard, he gets angry and he runs upstairs... Once, he was, you know, ignoring me and I got really mad, I went up the stairs and I kicked the door and he was like, he ran up the stairs, said, "What are you doing? What are you doing?" I'm like, "Yeah, yeah." I was telling him, I said, "You always..." I cursed at him, like, "I f---ing hate you." Then, when I said that, he spanked me. You know, he slapped me a couple times in the head. He threw me on the bed, he put me under the covers and he was like, "You stay in here for the rest of the day and night." I fall asleep. That's it. "You're punished, stay here," and this and that. That was the end of that.

You know, that happened so many times I can't even... you know, that's one incident I really remember a lot, because the way he really hit me hard when I was upstairs. Like, he was pounding on my, you know, on my head and my back and he was like, "Why you do that? Why you do that?" I don't know, he was always strict. Strict, you know, with punishment as strict, you know, he used to hit me, too, physically. Physically and mentally, you know? He used to be strict.

HE RAISED ME

I mean, yeah, he raised me. He taught me most of the things I know. I mean, he taught me how to play soccer. He taught me how to, you know, stand up for myself. Don't ever let another person run over you, you know? If you feel you're right, you know, don't ever let another person bring you down.

He used to encourage me all the time, you know? He's always telling me, you know, "Protect your little sister in school." You know, he used to be like, he used to give me pride. He used to give me confidence. He used to tell me, "Don't let this and this do this to you. Don't let them, you know, watch out with who the people you mess with." He taught me lots of things, he taught me, you know, the basics—brush my teeth, take a shower. He did what everyone's father does, you know, for his son.

GRANDMA

My grandma used to spoil me the most. My dad used to give me things too, right, when I really wanted them. But my grandma was the one that used to spoil me a lot. She lives in Queens, where I'm at right now. She's this really happy old lady, you know? She's... I think she's like 60 – no, she's 70. I think she's 70 now. She's still... I don't know, every time

Magic

she sees me, she gets real happy. That's why I always see her as a happy person. I don't know, I never—when I'm not around, I don't know how she acts like. Every time I'm around, she's happy. She really, you know, I know she really loves me and all that… She used to be buy me things… video games.

VIDEO GAMES

I like video games a lot. Those were a big part of my life and all that, you know? I love video games. I like RPGs, I like sports games. First and foremost, I like RPGs. Like now, I'm really into the MMORPGs… Final Fantasy. I started with VII, 'cause I was too young for the other ones in my time. I started with VII and then ever since VII, I went up, beat every other one. I don't know. I like the fantasy, you know, like the things that you can't do in real life, you can do them in videogames. Like, say you're playing Madden – I play a lot of Madden, too – there's a lot of things that you can't, you know, you can't be in the NFL. And you get to create your own players, you know, you get to go through the career and all that. I don't know, it's just… it's fun. It's fun. It's real fun. I don't know, it's like I could play all day. I could play since I wake up. Like, say I wake up at 8:00 in the morning. I'll play 'til 10:00 at night and fall asleep. I'll play the whole day. If I'm really into a game and I really want to beat it, I end up, you know, I end up playing the whole day… it's like I've been stuck in a trance for so long. I get out of my room, I go, you know, get something to drink, eat, you know, and maybe go outside for a little bit, and then go back to sleep and then wake up the next morning, see what other game I gotta beat. 'Cause I have a whole lot of games.

I bought my own computer, hooked up my room. I'm on a computer game, now, a lot. I got my XBox 360, my PS3, Wii. I've got everything. I got all my videogames all by myself. XBox, I've got about like fifteen, Playstation 3, I've got about ten, for the Wii I've only got like four. For the Playstation 2, I've got like 30 games. And from the original Xbox, I've got like ten games. So, I've got a whole stack. It's huge! Plus, I've got DVDs... It was really nice, you know? That's the part I miss the most, is my room, 'cause I worked on it so much.

Lately, before I came here, I stopped buying console games and started buying—I started playing this game World of Warcraft. I'm really into it, man. All my—it's not like, you know, regular Warcraft. It's like you have your own character, build them up... you know, you upgrade 'em. I got up to level 45. Like, max level is 70, and I got up to level 45 before I got here. And I was really good, like, it was like working on yourself but in an imaginary world. It's like where all these people—it's like ten million people around the world that play... It was just fantasy. It was like really huge, really cool, man. And the fact that all your friends are on—all, you know, on this one little thing, talking to each other, playing... you know, it's crazy. Technology, it's great.

MONEY

Outside I was, you know, I was outside. Like, right before I got locked up, I was selling drugs and all that, 'cause my parents... my parents wouldn't give me any more money. My grandma, she—I can't be taking money from them, 'cause they're in some sort of debt. I don't even know all about it, but they're in some sort of debt. So you know, I started making my own money and all that, I started buying my own things. So, I was selling drugs for a little while.

You know, I'm not proud of it, but I couldn't—I tried to get a job once and it like... I really applied at Best Buy. It was when I was back in high school. Well, I'm still in high school, 'cause I'm finishing high school here. I'm not doing the GED, I'm finishing high school. This was back when I was in high school, like two years – no, no, last school year, the beginning of last year, in August. I applied for Best Buy. When I applied, I got the job and everything.

I went to get the urine test, you know, everything was fine. But then they did a background check. I told them I ain't got convictions or nothing, but I had a case from February of the last year that I was still on the ACD on. So the ACD popped up and, you know, ACD means it's dismissed—it's just, you know, you're under supervision. So Best Buy, under the guidelines, they couldn't hire me.

So that really gave me like a pissed off, like the whole world's against me attitude. I thought I had a job and everything. I was happy, you know? I was ready. It would've been, you know, some days, 'cause I was playing football too, at the time. It'd been, you know, school or job, or school and football. You know, I had keep myself occupied everyday. I had the whole schedule planned out and everything, you know? ACD, I don't know what it stands for, but I know it's like, after your case is dismissed, after like you beat your case, you're not supposed to get in trouble for a certain amount of time. Mine was six months. Six months ACD, don't get in trouble and come back, you know, or your other case can be reopened. I remember getting the letter. I was so pissed off, you know? It was there, and it was like Best Buy. I thought it was something good. But it ended up being something bad.

The first court date, I went to after the date. The next court date, I beat it. It was like, "Oh, dismissal." The victims didn't show up. There was a big fight in front of a club, you know? It depressed me. I was like, man… I just gave up all hope on that and I kept going to school that year. I finished, you know? Right now, I'm in the 12th grade. I was in my 11th—that was in 11th grade. I hadn't gone to school for two years in a row, and just last year I blew the whole year. So it was like three years I didn't go to no school. I still could do it, 'cause I got 36 credits. I'm finishing it in here. By June, I should have my high school diploma. I passed all my regents except the math.

After the Best Buy incident, though, that's when I started selling drugs, 'cause I was like, "You know what, there's nothing," you know? The ACD was going on for the next four months, so I was like, "Forget about it," you know? My friend, he started giving me the drugs and all that. He was like, "Sell this and give me this much money back." Then, I got addicted to it. I just started making money and seeing how many video games, you know, I could buy.

ANOTHER CHANCE

Back in '04 I, ended up in C74 for a real serious case. I was there about two months. My mom bailed me out on a 50 thousand dollar bail. She put up the house and all that after two months. I was fighting the case from outside and, you know, I was really scared. I was ready to—they were offering me two to four years. I was really, really, really scared, and you know, I was about seventeen at the time. I was like, "Damn, I've never been in jail this long. You know, I don't want to do no two to four years."

So I was getting ready, prepared, you know? Whatever. It was going to be two-to-four years. That was the lowest offer that was given me. Then, the kid that had filed the complaint against me, he stopped going to court. He got caught up and did a robbery, so he stopped going to court, and that helped me, 'cause then after a while my case got dismissed. He didn't show up three times and my case was dismissed. That made me so happy.

I was like, oh, that has to be a message from God, you know? He decided to give me another chance. Now I can finish high school. So what I did, I went back to high school the next day, enrolled again. I started this when I was playing football. I mainly went back to high school to play football, but I was going to finish high school anyways.

So I went back to high school and all that, I joined the football team. My life was looking good for '05, you know, '06. But come '07, like the end of '06, going on '07, everything started downgrading again because they had took me off my medication. Everything started going down the hill again and I stopped going to school. I mean, I finished the year, the '06 year of school, but I started like, I don't know, just started – everything started, you know, messing up. Everything was – the medication had me focused and steady and on track. I made a routine, you know, I was going through every day. But once they took me off that, I started going back down again. Next thing you know, I end up here again. I'm here again right now. Now, I'm facing about three years.

FOOTBALL

When I was younger, I used to play football in Long Island. Like, touch with my friends or tackle at recess in elementary school. Organized football, I never really played until about '04. Bryant High School. I practiced with them, you know, I played with them. Fullback, halfback sometimes, linebacker sometimes. They would switch me out, you know... I was really in shape when I was – back in '05, I was 185. All muscle. I really wasn't like this. This had happened in less than a year. I'm going to tell you the truth, it's crazy. I got so big in less than a year. From selling drugs, you know, staying at home playing video games, eating all the time. That's what got me like this.

But those two years before that, I was always active. I was at school, then after school was out I practice, come home, eat, take a shower, and sleep. That used to be my routine every day. So I was always in shape. I wasn't big—I was about 185. I was real fast and I liked roughness, you know? I play tackling and all that. So, you know, football is the perfect sport for me. Still to this day, I dream of playing football. It'd be in my dreams. I still remember playing football and it pisses me off now because, you know, you're in here, you can't. I've got no chance to be out on a football team, on an outside league or something. So I don't know. Football taught me how to act like... a person, you know?

COACH HERNANDEZ

Well, Coach Felix was the one, you know? He used to put me in discipline. He used to be... I'm working out and all that, and I don't know, he just made me want to act like a... Like, I'll see how the captain's acting and all that, and I'll look up to them and act like them. They don't act like no a--h---s, you know what I mean? Pickin' on the weaker kid and that, you know?

Well, he used to do that all the time, 'cause I used to argue with the other halfback or the other fullback that, "No, let me go. It's my turn," and he would call me out and be like, "No, man, you've got to stop being greedy. You're not the only one on this team." He told me, you know, "You've got to stop wanting all the plays for yourself, 'cause you should run plays over and over. But I used to stay there and it used to be us and the other player, you know, "Come on, switch up." And I used to be like, "You know, wait, one more play." But he pulled me out and he was like, "You can't be doing that. You've gotta start learning how to act right. You've gotta give people their chance too, you know? You didn't come here starting, so they want to get their chance to shine, too." He told me how to basically not be so selfish or whatever you want to call that. I maybe wanted to listen, 'cause he was my coach and I looked up to him a lot, man. He was just... he's this guy that runs a crew of like 40 of us, this big team. And I look up to him, 'cause everyone else looks up to him. He got all of us under control, you know. I respect that. And, you know, he's the shot-caller and all that, you know? He just made me want to... I listened to whatever he said. He used to tell me anything and I'd listen to him.

Anything. I would never deny a workout that he would give me or anything. Most other kids would be like, "No, Coach, I don't want to do it." I'd be like, "Come on, all right. I'll even do extra."

BEST FOOTBALL MEMORY

That must've been like last – when I was nineteen, I was playing with friends against another team, when they played the Cougars. You know, it was like, it was the last TD we needed. We were like four yards away and I'm playing fullback and we needed this touchdown  to win. So, I get the ball and they do a play with me and it was – what was that called again? A counter, it was a counter, inside hand-off counter to the C-pocket – that means the right. No, no, the B. Yeah, the C.

So, I got the ball, I made to pretend I was going to the B-hole… I went to the C-hole, you know? And when I just looked up, nobody was there. I see one guy there and I run right over him and I'm making this touchdown and we win the game. I don't know, ever since, I've – that was like one of the best memories I have for football. All the pressure was on me and everything. It was a rush. And when you did it, you feel so proud, like, "Oh man."

PRESSURE

The pressure? I like it… but sometimes I don't, you know? Sometimes it messes me up, but… it could mess me up or it could give me more strength, you know? 'Cause you're under pressure and you're nervous. Pressure, I mean, I prefer being in the game without pressure, you know, like, we're winning from the beginning of the game. This pressure, you know, is nothing to me. You know, it's just going to either make me mess up or it'll make me stronger. Like I said, it's nothing big, you know?

TOUGHNESS

Roughness? When I was younger I used to be real... when I used to get hit by my dad, I used to, I don't know, I used have aggression towards him and all that. So, I used to go to school all the time mad and pissed off. I'd take it out on the other kids, bullying them, you know? And, I don't know, I always ended up fighting, and I... liked it. It was something that, you know... if you lose, it's horrible, you know? If you lose a fight? But if you win, you feel real good about yourself. Mostly, at the same time, I used to feel bad for the other kid or whatever, but it was something that was just part of me, and I just liked it.

I'm an angry guy, you know? But I started playing football. I learned how to control that aggression and use it on the field. When I was in school and I played football all the time, I never even got into a fight, never argued with people. I was always, you know—it really straightened me out.

RANDY

This one kid... I didn't like too much. I was, like, about ten and this kid, he throws a ball—not dodge ball—kickball. He was bigger than me and everything, he wasn't no kid that was a threat to anybody. He was, you know, he was a good kid. But he wanted to play around with me and then he threw a ball at me. When he threw the ball at me, I got real angry. I went up to him and I kicked him and I punched him in the rib, I punched him in the face.

Magic

He got real hurt. The next thing I know, he's on the floor, he's crying and all that. He's calling the staff, the teachers over there. I'm like… I feel sorry for him, 'cause all the other kids are like, "Why'd you do that?" or the other. And I'm thinking to myself, "Yeah, why did I do that? You know, you were just playing around. I could've thrown the ball back." But I felt sorry for him, 'cause he was there laying on the floor, crying and holding his rib and all that. And I felt bad for him.

That had got me in a lot of trouble with his parents, 'cause his parents had sent detectives to my house or something like that to talk to my parents. They sent police to the house, you know, "You've got this kid, he can't be abusing this kid" or something. I don't know what really happened—I was too young to understand. But I know they sent police to my house over that. I really got in trouble. I felt bad for the kid after that. I bruised up his ribs and all that. You know, I don't why… I just feel bad. There was a blackout 'cause there was an instant reaction. It's like, "Why the hell'd you hit me with the ball?" and I'm coming out at this kid that don't really do nothing to nobody, so it's surprising, so it just, like, blacked me out.

BLACKOUTS

I used to black out arguing with my stepfather. I used to just say wild things. That's why it used to get me usually beat or punished. Now that started happening when I was like, ten, twelve.

LONG ISLAND AND NEW YORK CITY

I'm from Valley Stream. That's by Green Acres Mall off of Sunrise Highway. So right there—the borderline of Queens and Long Island. So many people. There's a lot of kids that act tough. In Long Island, we were the tough kids. Everybody knew that we were the tough kids. Me and my little group that we used to have, you know… we were all the same age. We used to be the kids—even with the older kids in our neighborhood, we used to fight with them all the time. We used to, you know, we used to run things around Long Island. Nobody would mess with us. We used to get all the girls and all that.

But it's like, here in the city was different for me, 'cause I was alone, you know? A lot of kids in the city act tough, so when I first came to the city, I got into a couple of fights. I got jumped, I jumped, I've beaten up kids one-on-one, kids have beaten me up one-on- one. You know, it's crazy, 'cause in the city everything went nuts. I didn't know nobody and I had to get my respect, so I was showing that by fighting a lot, you know?

I mean, kids in the neighborhood, when they hear about you… like, you started beating this guy and this guy up and they hear that you're beating all the cats up around the neighborhood. I mean people started, you know, "Oh, who's this kid, Magic?" all that, you know? It was nothing, nothing big to me. I just wanted to earn my same respect that I used to have in Long Island in my neighborhood, you know, with my group of friends and all that.

It was just so people, you know, when they look at me they don't look at me like some sort of… some sort of punk or sort of wussy. I ain't no, you know… I look at other people like they're a weaker link, you know? But I got abuse out of me, you know, a long time – like I told you, I started playing football. I started growing up after that. After sixteen, I started, you know?

Magic

DOWNHILL

I started drinking a lot, started not caring anymore. Just been pissed off all the time. I started eating to take away my depression and all that. I was doing bad and then, you know, I was like, "I want money." It just gave me ambition to get money, 'cause I needed money, you know? For my needs. I wanted food, I wanted video games, I wanted to do what I wanted to do. So, I started selling drugs. I never got caught for selling drugs though, you know? I'm not planning to neither. And I'm not planning to sell drugs when I get out of here neither.

HIGH SCHOOL DIPLOMA

Well, it means to me... I'm not saying anyone can't get a GED, you know? You have to be smart to get a GED, too, but a high school diploma to me feels like you need to struggle more, 'cause you need your Regents, you need to pass your finals at the end of the semesters. I don't know, it just makes me feel better. It makes me, when I say 'high school diploma,' it just makes me feel better, you know? All these kids in here doing GED, I'm the one doing high school diploma. I mean, there's like two other kids doing high school diploma, too. But it makes me feel better, you know. I don't know... I can't explain it.

THE FUTURE

Well, I want to do a lot of things. When I was really in shape back in '06, the beginning of '06 and '05, I wanted to be a gym teacher. I was planning to go to grad school and all that. I had a plan and everything. I was going to go to Nassau Community College. I was going to play football there for, you know, two years. Then, I'll go to whatever school after that, play another two years and do, you know, whatever courses you need to do to become a teacher. Then go to grad school for a teacher, you know? But, I mean, everything went downhill and plans didn't work out. I wanted to be a gym teacher. Really. Now what I'm looking forward to is being a nurse or an actor.

ACTING

Being an actor's my priority, but you gotta go through a lot to be an actor. When I was younger, did elementary school plays and all that. I did the Christmas... the kings, the three kings. I mean, the kings, when they bring Jesus all his presents. See, when I was younger, I was in Catholic school, too. I was one of the kings in the play. What else... I was... I forgot what reindeer I was in something like, with Santa in a Christmas parade. I was a reindeer... I don't know. I don't really remember it. I just remember being in a play. I mean, I had one with a float, when I was young young, really young. It is interesting, but I mean, it is an interest area, but it's a lot of work. You have to have very good memory for the scripts and all that. My memory is, you know, if you tell me—if you give me something to remember and you know, you're giving me a couple bucks and all that, I'm going to definitely remember it.

I'm interested in the way people—the way actors—make themselves seem in movies, you know what I mean? Like, let's say if I see somebody in the street, it gives an actor that, you know, that look and the fame and all that. That must feel real good, all these people knowing you and all that. The way the actors, you know, like let's say, you know Al Pacino? When he worked on Scarface? You see Al Pacino now and, you know, you're going to be like... everyone giving him respect, his fame. That must feel real good. That's why I don't like feeling bad, you know? I like feeling good about myself. So, you know... The money's good, too, just 'cause I like it, I don't know. Like, I like acting out other personalities, other people.

Magic

BEING BIPOLAR

Also, I want to be a nurse and even though I know I have a mental disorder—bipolar disorder and all that—I know there's other people that have it way more severe than me. So, I wanted to be a nurse in, like, mental institutions or somewhere, working with those kind of people and helping them out, you know? See, I know how it feels, kind of. I know bipolar is a bad—you know… it's like horrible. You could be happy one day for like two hours and then, next thing, you go all the way to the bottom and feel like crap, just from one little thing.

What's bad is the mood swings are so crazy and like, they go from one to another mood in seconds. When I was in that evaluation center back when I went to juvenile detention center when I lived in Long Island, they evaluated me there and they diagnosed me bipolar.

I monitor myself. Now that I have to – the past couple of years I've been seeing like, I've been taking medications and watching what my medications do to me, how they make me react and all that. I know which medications work for me, and I know some don't. Some of them are controlled substances, so I can't get them here.

I want to give back, you know? I want to help all those people that… mental health, something's mental, you know? It's not like… you know, you can have a physical disorder and it's something that you can take away. I wish people knew that, you know? Once you're born with mental health problems, you're stuck with it for the rest of your life. And that's really sad. You know what I mean? I wish more people knew that, and this country put more into working with people like that, and research more up on mental health things and helped the mental health people. Because what they're going through—they have no clue what the people that have mental problems are going through. It's torturing sometimes. It's torturing, torturing, torturing.

DEPRESSION

The depression that I get—bipolar's another way of saying manic depression, and it gets real bad. Like, when I broke up with my girlfriend, it got real bad. This was back when I had just moved out here, the end of 2003 or 2004. I broke up with my girlfriend from Long Island and found out that she had another boyfriend and all that. That really got me real down, you know?

So, I'm living already in Queens then. I started going outside a lot to forget about her. I started drinking a lot, getting into fights. This was how everything started. It's just bad, man, 'cause it can get you in trouble. Some people, it takes them to their grave, 'cause they actually go to that extra limit and do suicide. I mean, I never have suicidal thoughts, but it really gets you down, man. It doesn't—it's something you don't want to live with, man. It's just… it's so horrible. You know, it still to this day bothers me I broke up with her. I still love her, you know what I mean? Still to this day, I feel a little depressed. It's something that sticks with you. It's not ever, ever, ever going to leave, no matter how… nah, you ain't gonna forget.

In the day that I broke up with her, I came outside and I was smoking packs and packs of cigarettes, one after another. And my friend's like, "What's going on with you, man?"

He's telling me, "Man, get over that girl." Specifically, he said to, "Get over that b----," you know, "Forget about it." I'm like, "You know what, man? You don't know what I'm going through," all that. After a while, I just shut up and I was like, "Yeah, yeah, whatever." I agreed with him just so he could shut up, 'cause you know,

Magic

you don't want to hear that. "Just get over it." I don't know, it's just not that easy, man. It's hard. It's hard, man. It's hard. You know, people think that men are usually the ones that should get up and get, you know, get over with it, but it's not like that. I don't really show—maybe the first couple days, you'll see me drinking, you know, when I have a fight with my girlfriend or I break up with them. Like smoking and all that. But I don't really show it. I don't show it when I'm around people. When I'm around people, I'm like a whole different person... but still, inside, you know, back in my head, it's still there. So it doesn't really affect, me 'cause nobody really points that out about me. I don't show it around people.

I feel weaker. Like mental, I feel like a man's supposed to be a man. He ain't supposed to be depressed, you know? You're supposed to be tough, and, you know, stick through it. It's something I can't avoid. I can't avoid it. If I get depression, it just comes to me. It's not something you can avoid or stop. It makes me feel weaker, to tell you the truth... 'cause it's not a 'disability', but it is a big-time disability. And a lot of other people have it. I'm not the only one that got it.

Feeling alone with it... it's bad, because I'm not the type to show it. I don't like talking about it. Like, to my friends, I don't really talk about it. I used to go to see doctors, you know? Psychiatrists and all that. I didn't want to... I wouldn't even tell them. I'd just talk about something else, like how's my day been going, how's my week been going. I wouldn't talk about what's really eating me up, you know, about girls, all that. Certain things in my life that, you know – mainly it was the girl, like, my girlfriends. That eats me up, you know? That's something I don't talk about, something I've got to go through myself. But like I said, it never leaves you.

I'D LIKE PEOPLE TO LEARN

I'd like people to learn that it's never too late. Do what you want to do in life. You know, don't flush it down the drain by going down to those low levels that maybe other friends tell you to do. Like, to be somebody that rob people, you know? Do what you want to do in life. Even though you know that you're young and you're supposed to do it, just stick through it. Just don't give up. Just keep going. Don't... not for anything—once you see a sign, a little thing that's taking you off track, try to correct it. Try to correct that and stay on track, you know? Don't fall off track. It's never too late, man. Never too late, you know, to try to do your best. For me... finish school. Go to college. You know, get a career, man, instead of being in this dump, you know?

I know it's not going to go good for me. It's my first time really doing that much time, but it's not... it wouldn't go good for anybody. You don't want to be in here, man. You know, there's no freedom here. There's only... you can't do what you want to do. It's not worth it.

Anything that you're about to do, think about it. Hopefully what I say, if you read this, moves you to think about it when you're about to do something bad, not to do it. Because once you're in here, you're in here. That's it, you've done the crime. You know, it's not like a bad dream, you ain't gonna wake up out of it.

When I'm sleeping I think that when I wake up... I'm thinking that it's a dream for a second, and then I'm trying to wake up out of it, you know. But this is really where you are, man, and this is where you're stuck. You know, it could be whatever. It could be a year, it could be 90 days, it could be 30 days. It's still taking away time from your life, you know what I mean?

They said I'm facing three years, but that ain't nothing compared to what other people are facing. But to you, it'll mean something, 'cause you know that maybe you didn't do it or

Magic

maybe you shouldn't have done it. But just… think twice. That's the message, you know, that I'm saying. That I'm trying to send out. I'm really trying to send out a message like, it's little things—don't let little things turn into big things that mess your life up.

One of the ways these small problems that turn into big problems had an impact on my life was the way it reflected on my sister. She wrote her college essay on my 'misfortune'… ADHD, bipolar disorder, criminal record, dropping out of school and getting kicked out of the house. Even though that was my past.

Always have confidence in yourself, self-esteem, and you'll get somewhere. That's the way it is, you know? Every time an adult talks to you, listen. Like, I'm saying it now, but when I used to be younger I used to say, "Nah, they all say that." But it's true, what the adults tell you, man. You know. Some people you got to listen to. They're wiser and they've been through more. That's basically all I can say, man.

Struggling Times Comes Hard Times

El Gringo

My name is El Gringo and I was born in Puerto Rico on September 30th, 1986.

EL MORRO

I had good times in Puerto Rico. I mean, I went to someplace called El Morro which is in San Juan and I've been pretty much everywhere. I've been to the old San Juan, which is antique. Growing up in Puerto Rico is hard. The lifestyle in Puerto Rico is not the same as here. It's like it's a poor place. I mean, it is good in some ways but money-wise, it's not good. You get paid minimum wage no matter what. If you have an education, well, then you get a little bit more but it's not New York. New York would pay you nine, ten, eleven dollars. In Puerto Rico, the minimum wage is five-fifteen, but you also don't pay taxes so it helps in some ways. In one way it works, but in another way it really doesn't come out to be, plus rent, plus this, plus that... especially if you've got kids.

VIOLENCE

Then you got the street part. You got violence out there. In Puerto Rico, they don't play around. Everything you find is bodies everywhere. They be killing people everywhere. It's not good. Puerto Rico is a dangerous place but it also depends on who you hang out with. I mean, it's a good place for you to go visit, stay for a couple of months, but for you to actually live there for as many years as I've been living there, it's not good. Every friend that I have is dead 'cause of the streets and all that. I love my country. I love Puerto Rico. I was born and raised there. So in one way it's good, but then in another way it's bad.

Everything was good growing up. When I was small, my father used to be in the Army so I got to travel a lot. So that's one good thing. I've been to Germany, I've been to Washington. I lived in Tennessee for a couple years. My father was in the military, so we had to move around a couple of times, from here and there and so everything was good for a while.

SEPARATION

Everything was good until maybe I was fifteen years old, and then everything changed. My father broke up with my mother, and so everybody started going their separate ways and I started going my separate way too. I really didn't have the love that I was supposed to have as I was growing up. No one to talk to at all, so I had a couple of rough times.

When I hit fifteen or sixteen years old, my father came to New York. Then, say, after two years my mother met somebody. She had a boyfriend and he was my friend. He was an older guy and he was in his early 50s. This was my mother's boyfriend and he'd seen me since I was a baby. He had seen me grow up, and then I started working, doing my own thing, so I would call him, "Oh, where you at?" He's a messenger and a bill collector for a Toyota dealer and he had been with Toyota for 20 years. He would go to different buildings all around Puerto Rico and collect either cash, checks or personal documents from people who did not meet their car payments. For example, he would go to a person's house and, if they had not paid, he'd take away their car, you know, all that. Every time he would go somewhere—I lived in the second house, he lived in the fifth house—so every time he would go somewhere he would go in reverse and honk the horn, "Oh, you want to go with me over there?" I would ask my mother, "I'm going with him over there." I like to take the trip because I visited almost everywhere in Puerto Rico. So that's how I became friends with him.

My mother liked him and he was kind of family here. I kind of got mad at first, but then I was like, "You know what, let it be." I kind of got mad at my mom's 'cause it won't be the same between me and him. It wasn't the same, but it's like the love is still there. So now they're together, thank God! Thank God everything's beautiful. He treats my mother well. So everything is good. You know, I go to Puerto Rico sometimes and I stay at their house and he treats me like I'm his son. Something that my father hasn't done for years. But it's O.K. I got through it.

My father wasn't really in my life that much. He was there whenever I had problems on the street or something. He would be there 'cause he didn't want nothing to happen to me. But other than that, sometimes he wouldn't call or act like I needed a father. So I started getting close to my mother's boyfriend, and he was like my father and I used to talk to him. I couldn't really talk to my father like that 'cause he was here in New York and he would move around. I wouldn't know his phone number or nothing until one day he called. Like, let's say probably two years later he called and so that's how I got his number and that's how I ended up over here. I had kind of a little confrontation in the street in Puerto Rico, you know, so put two and two together. I didn't want nothing to happen to me or my family, so I decided to come out here to New York and live with my father for a little while.

GOOD TIMES WITH MY FATHER

Everything was good. Like, when I was little, when you're small what can possibly go wrong? When you're little, when you are at least six, ten years old, what can possibly go wrong? Everything is like gold to you. Your father gives you everything. Well, that's if you've got a father and a mother. But if you've just got your mother or you just got your father, they're going to treat you and at that age you're going to have everything. Your father's going to let you have sneakers and clothes on your back. He's going to take care of you. So everything was good, everything was beautiful. We would go out to places, like a movie theater, a father and son type of thing. Until I started getting a little bit older. When I started getting a little bit older, I had my first job at the age of fifteen. So then everything started to change.

I was working, I was making a couple of dollars at McDonald's by that time. That's my first job, McDonald's, and I stayed there for probably a year or two. Once you start working and once you start being independent then your father will be like, "Well, you're working." Well, you know, that's my father. He was like, "You're working, so you can afford... I already did my part." He figured that he already did his part for fifteen years, you know, so it's time for me to do my part. So that's how I started getting my own things. I started dressing the way I wanted to dress, not like cheap sneakers, cheap shirts, none of that. I wanted to dress how I wanted to dress. I wanted to have jewellery. I wanted to have my own hats. So little by little, I started buying my own things and so everything was pretty good until that point and age.

LIVING IN NEW YORK

It's a different environment. Like, in one way, it's good. I started working when I got

over here it's like there's a lot of money. In other words, it's nothing compared to Puerto Rico. The jobs are better, you get paid more. I was getting paid five-fifteen. My first job out here was a gas station, nine-fifty an hour, yeah, nine-fifty an hour for 40 hours. So every two weeks, I'd come home with almost seven hundred dollars, plus overtime.

When I came out here, I lived with my father and his girl. His girl, we didn't really get along but I accepted her because if I accepted my mother to have her boyfriend then I'm going to accept my father to have his girlfriend, even though I didn't feel that he should be with her. But it happens, and it's going to happen for a reason, so I accepted her. She used to buy me everything 'cause she got a good job and she liked everything expensive. That's one of the girls that I don't like, you know, how some people don't care what you have? But her, she like everything to be expensive. She got the money for it. I mean, she can go ahead and do it, you know? And then my father started being expensive too. He started dressing up, chains and everything, started getting in that lifestyle. I was like, that's not even my father, that's not him. He would waste money on stupid expensive stuff and not have money to at least take his son or take us somewhere.

Everything was good until I got out here. When I got out here and started living with my father, it was good at the beginning. You know, I'll say this… it was good at the beginning. So it's good for a couple months, almost a year, and then everything started getting ugly. I started fighting with her and everything started getting reckless until the age of eighteen. When I hit eighteen, I decided I'd move out. She kicked me out 'cause of my father's actions. She would have an argument with my father and she'd wake me up and she'd kick me out. She kicked me out three times and she would come back to me, "I'm sorry, I didn't kick you out." I said, "Okay," 'cause that's my father's girl so I was like, you know what, I'm going to give her another chance. She woke me up again, 6:00 in the morning. The third time, at the age of eighteen, I got my own apartment.

Gringo

MY FRIEND JOHNATHAN

I have one best friend. That friend, I could say that he's been with me through everything. That was the first person I met. I met him by my father's girl. They used to work with each other. They used to call him nephew, but he wasn't. So I got introduced to him and he was Puerto Rican too, so we kind of like bonded together.

My first job when I came to New York was a gas station in Staten Island called Mobile Underground. The second job was at the College of Staten Island and that's where I met him. Me and him stick together. We work together. We kind of bonded. We exchanged numbers. I'm 21 now, he's probably like 23. When we met each other, we was close so we started hanging out, started going to movie theaters, starting to go to Coney Island. We really clicked together. I quit that job. I got myself another job and then he quit that job. He got the same job as I did. We used to work at Minor League Yankee Stadium in the concession stands. I used to cook because at that time I wasn't old enough to pour beer 'cause I think you have to have over 21 to pour beer. So we got that job together. We was working there for three years in summertime and then after that seasonal job, I don't remember where else we used to work. But we used to work, I think, three or four jobs together, you know, that hired both of us on.

We used to do everything for years. We do everything together and by that time I didn't want to have nobody by my side. I didn't want to have no girlfriend. I didn't want none of that. By that time, I just wanted to do me, get work, get my own apartment before I start settling with somebody. That's all I wanted to do. Then Johnathan got a girlfriend, and he introduced me to her sister. So I started talking to the girlfriend's sister. We got along and we used to talk. She was my girlfriend by then, so it's like we did everything together. I moved out and he moved out and we lived in a place like a boarding house and they got little apartments.

He moved to one apartment and I moved downstairs to the same house in another apartment. Everything was good and we used to do stuff together. We used to go everywhere together and everything was lovely and then he left.

The only thing that broke my heart is that he left. He wanted to join the Army, so he wanted me to join the Army. But I didn't want to take the same footsteps as my father because I knew how it is. I know how all that Army thing goes. I mean, I was single, I could've done it 'cause I'm not married or nothing. But he decided to do it and I told him I didn't want to do it. I told him, "You do. Don't let me stop you. Don't let anybody stop you from what you want to do. You know, you want to go for the Army, go for the Army. Here's my number. I'm always going to be around. Trust me, I'm always going to be around." Someday, if it's meant to be, we're going to meet up together. You know, someday we'll cross each other, if it's meant to be.

FOND MEMORIES OF PUERTO RICO

Oh man! One of the memories that I had that I loved was… well, it started like this. There was a little get together. I don't remember if was Christmas, Thanksgiving, I don't remember exactly what event was it but it was like a little get together. I hadn't seen my cousins in years, so I was happy that I was going to be seeing my cousins from Florida that I hadn't seen for God knows how long. We all met up at this one hotel. One of my aunts had a friend who rented out apartments and he owned the whole complex. So on that day we had one floor and, like, he didn't rent it out to us out. He let us have four apartments where everybody was having fun all day. So everybody got together and it just happened to be that as soon as you walked out of the complex, there was a swimming pool and if you walked out of that swimming pool, the beach was right there. Everything was good. We had fun, I drank

Gringo

too. We just had our own fun. We played dominos, we played cards, we bugged out. It was nice 'cause we had a little get together with my family. I think that was probably the last get together that the whole family got 'cause little by little then my grandmother started dying, my grandfather died, you know. So that's probably the last thing that I remember when everybody was united. It was good.

The only thing bad about that one day was I went to the beach, and we was playing dominoes out there the whole day. Then my family decided that the next day we're going to celebrate at the pool. So we paid for the pool. We closed the pool down and it was only a family get together. So the next day we had like a little pool party. The only thing that I got out of that is I got a third-degree burn. Yeah, sunburn! So it was good. It was good at one time, but then that little incident that I had to go to the hospital but I didn't care 'cause it was very good. That's probably one of my fondest memories.

RODOLFO'S POOL HALL: A PLACE TO REMEMBER

A place that I remember is called Rodolfo's. It's a pool hall that I used to go to chill, smoke, I mean doing pretty much what everyone does. So I used to go over there and chill with my mans. We used to get a little get together and we just used to go over there. That was one of the places that I used to always go to if my friend was bored. Me and him used to go over there so that's why that place is really important to me. I would just go there and we would chill and get maybe two or three tables for the people that used to go. Get two or three tables at the very corner and we would just chill you know, have fun. It's better than being out there on the streets, out there for trouble, so we would just go there being bored. Let's say one Saturday we got no place to go, we just used to go there. We used to drink, smoke, because back there you are allowed. It's not like you are allowed to smoke but we was cool with the dudes there, the bouncers there, so we were allowed to smoke. So that's pretty much what I used to do. We used to chill until late, three or four o'clock in the morning and everybody got bored and everyone used to go home. We used to go and play pool. There's a couple of like fights that we used to get in. That's 'cause other people would start 'cause they think that they are better than us. You know how it is when you get together with your little crew. You are kind of twisted, you know, so it's just like somebody will say something to you while you are having fun and it ruins the whole excitement.

Rodolfo's is beautiful. It has like fifteen pool tables. You got the DJ in one corner,

the bathroom in another corner and it's like as soon as you walk in it's the bar. In the back area you got the pool halls—you got like ten to fifteen pool tables—so everything is good. It's nice and clean. It's neat and everything is fresh. It's new. You got the pool sticks is new, everything is neat. That's why I like going there. The people that go there, yeah, you got everybody that goes there. It's not like you got a spot where kids hang out. You got a lot of people that's older, a lot of adult people, either with their wife or whatever. Occasionally, you got other children, you got other people that comes to the spot too.

GRANDMOTHER VIRGINIA

My grandmother lives in Puerto Rico. That's my grandmother from my father's side. She's just like me. She's blonde, she got green eyes, freckles and that is the grandmother that

Gringo

was most close to us—me and my brothers—growing up and everything. You know, so it's like we go travel with her.

With her, everything was good. She used to give us treats, she used to give us money. She owned two houses. It's like a little dead-end and she owned the house on the right and the house on the left. On the back of the houses, they got a trail that you keep going and both of them meet together. So she had everything set up. She had flowers, she had her own garden. She had a tree called aguacate, avocado tree. Yeah, that's very famous in Puerto Rico, you know, and some fruit called acerola. That's a different… it's like a little cherry but it's not a cherry, you know? It's the same size and everything but it's very sweet. So they got that out there. Also quenepa. She had everything back there. Me and my brothers used to go climb up on the tree and pick out the ones that were ready. Sometimes we'll sell them to our little neighbours and sometimes we would just munch on them.

So that part, from my grandmother, it was lovely. And then she died in 2003, I think it was. Her heart exploded. She was probably like 70, 60-something. It was on a Mother's Day. Very sad because we were all supposed to get together that day at my aunt's house in Puerto Rico. It happened that my father's cell phone was ringing, ringing, ringing, and ringing and they called him to work and it was an emergency. "All right, I'll go to work," and they paid him double. He preferred the money 'cause we were on a tight budget, you know. Next thing you know, it ended up that she died and that was the first time in a long time that she got dressed up in a white dress, makeup and everything. She died on Mother's Day.

GRANDFATHER JOSE-PEPE

My grandfather from my mother's side, he was like 80-something years old. He's the one that took care of me, and he had seen me as soon as I was born. He was the one that cleaned me up, washed me. My grandfather was closely attached to me and not so much with my big brother and my little brother.

My grandfather had a lot of problems health-wise. He was diabetic, his sugar was high and he had a lot of stuff. So after a few years, he fell one time and that one time led him to be in a wheelchair for life. No feelings in his legs whatsoever because of that one fall 'cause his bones was weak and supposedly he broke his two legs as soon as he fell. He used to be in a wheelchair, so I'd take him to the balcony and he couldn't walk but if he held onto something he would drag his feet a little bit. He would try. That's one thing about my grandfather that, no matter what, he wasn't just like some people would be. Some people would just stay in a wheelchair and be like, "Oh, my life is over because I can't walk." My grandfather wasn't like that. He would be like, "You know, while I'm going out to the balcony I'm going to do exercise." So he'd struggle to get up and he would walk to one corner and then he'd have to walk back because there's nobody there to help him. That's how it made him a little bit stronger and stronger because you figure that you go out to the balcony and you say, "I'm going to walk five steps to the side," you gotta walk five steps back and sit down on the wheelchair because if you walk five steps to the side, I guess you just gonna stand there until somebody comes to help you. So he really forced himself and that's one good thing about my grandfather. He was always forcing himself to do more than what he could do, I'll say even if he was in the wheelchair or not, you know.

Then my grandfather, he fell again, and that's when he started like... I guess he pinched a nerve or two nerves or something. That happened years ago, so I don't know what exactly went on. He fell again off his bed. He had blood everywhere and he lost a lot of blood. That's when everything started getting worse and worse and worse. He was in bed with machinery in my house 'cause he didn't want to be with the doctors. It's like he was in the hospital for two or three months but once they think you're getting a little bit better, then your family can take care of you.

I remember I felt bad. I would see him and I would cry because he would have tubes. He couldn't even use the bathroom or nothing. Everything was by cables. I'd see so much machines, knowing that it's the only thing keeping him alive. It's like a plug. You plug in the machine and it starts up everything. So it's like what would happen if... I always thought like what would happen if the electricity got cut off or what would happen if there's a blackout and there's no power, you know what I'm saying? And my house didn't have no generator 'cause, remember, Puerto Rico's a poor place. Not a lot of houses had generators. My house, I used to take a cold shower so that's why I got used to cold and this is not a problem for me. I always thought of what would happen 'cause in Puerto Rico sometimes the electricity goes out because it's an island so sometimes you get like... I mean, there's a couple of hurricanes but there's no cold. It never snows, it never gets cold. It's always hot. 100 degrees all year long. Sometimes we would have wind and this thunderstorm and sometimes it's too weak, wherever the electricity's coming from, sometimes it's too weak and so our electricity cuts off.

So I always thought what would happen if I woke up tomorrow morning and over the night the electricity cuts off 'cause sometimes it would happen. We wouldn't cook for days because of that. What would happen if the next thing you know, I wake up in the morning and my grandfather's dead because of that? So, I felt really bad seeing him with machinery and all that. I think he was on machinery for like a year, year-and-a-half, almost two years. They took the machinery off and he started breathing on his own. He could breathe by himself. So everything, it's like it shifted back to the same way that he was in a wheelchair. Just because of that one fall because elderly people, when they fall, it's like it seems that something else is wrong with them. So, to see him bad, it's crazy to see him with a lot of machinery.

MY COUSIN JENNIFER

Then I lost my cousin Jennifer who was the next closet cousin that passed away. Her death was also traumatic for me because these were my family. So this is how I felt about my cousin and the situation she was in.

She was here in New York and I don't remember what hospital in Manhattan. Supposedly, when she was born the doctor pulled her but pulled her too hard and broke her spines. Broke everything. The doctor broke everything on the little girl. She was in the hospital all her life, 23 years. One, she didn't talk so 23 years without talking, 23 years without moving. And 23 years without eating, only everything is by tubes and she couldn't get up. They would bathe her, like they do in the hospital, with little sponges. They would move her here and there but, physically, she couldn't move her herself. She couldn't move. If she wanted something, like if she wanted something to drink, she'd blink once. Or if she wanted something to eat, like to feed her through the little tube or whatever, she would blink twice and so everything would be by blinks. The faster you do it, like she would blink five times means something else. That's how her mother and her communicated for 23 years every day, pretty much every day. I would come up and see her in the hospital and she would smile at me but seeing her like this was very painful and heartbreaking. I wouldn't want to see a family member in the hospital as long as she was. Every time I looked at her, I could tell and you could see it in her eyes that she was in so much pain. She died and now she is in a nice place watching over us. She died in 2006.

BOCA AND ME IN PUERTO RICO:
STRUGGLING TO SURVIVE AND LIVING A PARANOID LIFE

I was in Puerto Rico and there came a point in time where it's just… I started doing bad, as in street stuff, as in robbing. All that stuff that you ain't even supposed to be doing. It's just like I started robbing, robbing motorcycles, you know, all that. I was doing it with… well, actually, I had another close friend.

The close friend that I had, his name was Boca. Boca in English means "mouth" 'cause he got big lips. That's why I used to call him that. Only me 'cause me and him was very close. So he used to steal. He used to steal motorcycles on the side. It's like we wouldn't steal them from people. We would just go to the airport and take them from the airport. I mean that's back then but it's like I got into that and that's why my mother said, "Don't trust anybody that's around you 'cause the dude that's around you is going to be a bad influence or maybe if you choose somebody good…" but I didn't know that at the time. Boca, yeah, he was a bad influence but he was my friend. In other words, we used to do good stuff. It's not all the time we used to do this. It just came across at one time we would be chillin' then see something and say I like that, so I took it. It's just like that mentality was reckless back then. Boca was one of my cool, my close friends.

If you rob from the wrong dude and you don't know who you're robbing from, they're going to come at you. That's what happened with my friend. He happened to rob the wrong dude. Now that dude was getting at us. So, in Puerto Rico, they don't talk. Over here they

can fistfight, you get off with a couple bruises. You get jumped, whatever it is. Over there, they'll kill you. See, in Puerto Rico, they don't play. They don't play none of that. They don't fistfight no more. They don't cut you off. They just shoot you, in front of cops or not. That's how everything is about survival over there. You've gotta watch who you talk to. You've gotta watch who you hang out with and, to tell you the truth, I got shot at a couple of times already. My struggle would be that I was surviving. I had to survive.

My mother moved out somewhere else, and my grandmother was alone so it's just like we didn't really have the type of stuff that a house should have. I started making money on the side to put my house, or my grandmother's house, up-to-date 'cause it was a poor house. You know, other people got their houses right. I'm living in a house where it's rains just once and the house leaks. It's cracked. You've got to put a cooking pan in front. That's how Puerto Rico is. So I started doing my thing so I can get enough money so I can put a whole roof up, little by little.

You grab a motorcycle and it depends who wants them how much they're going to give you. One of the newest motorcycles that came out, I got one of those and I got six grand for it. So it's just me and my friend, "Hey, you get three thousand dollars and I get three thousand dollars." But little by little, I kept on making more money and more money and then I started buying stuff for the house. Then I used to buy other things that I'm not supposed to buy, plus drugs or whatever it is. The reason why I started getting into that lifestyle was just because of the money, I guess, 'cause I was making a lot of money stealing. I was making a lot of money, so I guess it's just about the money or whatever, you know. When it came to that point, like I didn't care. Like it is, what it is. That was what I had in my mind. If I got killed, I got killed. I did my dirt, I did my thing, that's how I always took it at.

Of course, no matter how real you're going to be, your heart is always going to be pounding when it comes to something like that. It's not being scared and otherwise, but you will get nervous. You don't know what to expect next. You don't know if you are going to die crossing the road. There's going to be somebody underneath that car who is going to

Gringo

shoot you up. You don't know none of that. You don't know what the next man is thinking. I was nervous and I used to walk around like this, like with my eyes all wide open. Before I cross the street I know all four angles, on the back of me, on the side of me, in front of me. I looked everywhere. You live a paranoid life, in other words. When you get shot at, when you get something like that, especially in Puerto Rico, you're going to live paranoid. That's how I lived for a couple of years. I was living paranoid.

To tell you the truth, all this changed when me and my mans, Boca, we was at a corner smoking. There's this car that comes by. I tell my mans, "Yo, get ready to run because I think these are the people that was looking for you and me." They pulled down the window, take out four guns. The next thing you know, I ran. By the time I looked back, I yanked him a little bit so he could run after me but it's like he got stuck, like he got paranoid. His feet wouldn't move. So I took off. Once I turned around. I took off maybe like half a block and I turned back and all I saw is they shooting at him and he dies. So they kill my mans. They kill my mans! Like, in other words, I see my mans go down, my best friend. I see my best friend go down. So I started thinking, I started changing. I changed a little bit. I still got a few things, everybody's still going to have a few things, but I'm trying to make myself better. That's when everything started changing.

Then one of my mother's friends called my mother and she drove an hour-and-a-half to the block were the incident was. He told my mother, "Oh, your son just got shot at. I seen him running. They're going to kill him," this and this and that. So then my mother came down and she started screaming. She was scared. She started crying. I see my mother crying, I see my stepfather crying and that broke my heart. This happened recently, about two years ago. This is why I'm in New York now 'cause my mother was begging me to go back to my father. Even though me and my father, we wasn't cool at the time. Me and him was not talking. We had a little confrontation over the phone and in the end I wasn't talking. But I was like, you know what, I'm going to do it for my mother because I wouldn't want her to miss out 'cause I know how that is. This is why I'm in New York now. It's not because I'm scared. For me, I don't care. I did it because my mother loves me 'cause maybe I don't love myself. I did it because my mother loves me and she don't want to see one of her sons go down. I decided to listen to my mother and I came out here so I could start changing. I felt bad because it's like my heart like… what I wanted to do was I wanted to kill all four of them in the car. That was my intention, you know what I'm saying? But what would I get out of that? I'd just get four bodies. You don't get really nothing out of that.

I felt bad when my mans went down but deep down inside of me I'm like, "Well, maybe God put him instead of me." Or maybe because he had no more future, maybe because he wasn't gonna succeed, He gotta sacrifice that body to help another soul. It's like He probably sacrificed him to help me out because He knows that I'm going to do good. He knows that maybe I'm going to succeed. He knows that I'm going to grow old. At that time, at that moment, I felt bad. To tell you the truth, I felt bad. I got so red. I got mad, tears started coming down because that's my mans, you know? That's one of my mans that was close. And really I don't say best friends because best friends would be somebody that leads you to the right way. He led me through the wrong way but that was back then, what could I say? You know, whatever is done is done. The only thing I could do now is try to switch my whole life over and try to make everything good out there. Everything's gotta come out good.

A PLACE TO GET AWAY AND THINK

A place I used to go and think is a park around my grandmother's way. You cross the street where my grandmother is and it's like you could see the bridge of San Juan that crosses into the airport. From that point of view, you can see everything and there is a little passageway. As soon as you walk inside the park, you got little things for little kids. You got little swings, or something, and then you keep walking and there is a trail and it's right around the edge. You got the water… you see the water on the other side and as soon as you keep walking you will pass underneath the bridge. Let's say you keep walking for half an hour, twenty minutes, you will pass underneath

the bridge and that's supposed to be the so-called famous San Juan bridge. The one that crosses you into San Juan.

I liked it so much because I used to just go there and think. I used to smoke at the same time but it keeps me away from everything and it's just like I used to go there and really think about how everything might be. Like, how to change myself, how to get out of this, you feel me? Like I said earlier, you know once you making good money that's all you care about… and it's not making a little money, it's making a lot of money. Once you make a lot of money, it's like money keep coming to you so you really don't care. You are making a lot of money and you don't want to give it up.

There's a spot. As soon as you walk further in, as soon as you walk fifteen minutes further into the trail, there is a rock. You climb on top of the rock and you just sit on a corner and you got trees on both sides. In Puerto Rico, there's a lot of iguanas. When I used to go over there, I would see a lot and I would start chasing them. I would start gaining on them because in Puerto Rico I used to raise them. I used to raise a lot of roosters and everything, you know. I would see a little bit on the other side. You can't see too much but, like from the ferry to Manhattan, you can see buildings. You can see everything. That's how it was in Puerto Rico, you know. You could see everything on the other side, plus you could see the bridge of San Juan. If I would have kept walking a little bit further, I would be under the bridge 'cause I lived as soon as you get off of the bridge of San Juan. That's where I lived.

I felt good when I sat on the rock. It's just like when you got this favorite spot... some people got a spot where they used to go and read. It's nice and quiet. You don't got nobody  like, nobody around and you just sit there and you think about everything that is going on. I have had different situations where I just needed to go there. Where I would just think, and look at the children running around with their mother and their father. One day I would like to have children or a child, so there's a lot of things you see that pushes you to think and pushes you to realize that you are going to be looking at death. You keep on doing this, you are going to get killed or something really bad is going to happen to you. So it's not all about just money and all that. To tell you the truth, I would just go there and think and it was good at the moment. But as soon as I got out of that spot and come back home, there is always somebody knocking on my door or coming with a car, come to pick me up, one of my friends. I am not going to let one of my friends down so that's the only problem. We used to go chill and that moment it's like... for me it didn't go to waste 'cause I always keep it in my heart but it's like in other words it went to waste 'cause you are still doing what you are doing. So no decision has been made. Basically, it's like at that particular moment you would like to think instead

Gringo

of going out there and shooting somebody or doing what you are doing, you know? You just used to go there and just think.

My thinking has been changing a little bit, plus I go to school. I'm going to school now. So little by little, it's changing me. It's just like I left that stop. I don't do what I used to do. I don't smoke no more. I don't do no drugs whatsoever. I left that all behind.

MY SCHOOL EXPERIENCE

I went to elementary school in Puerto Rico, a school called Evangelico. I was there for a couple of years and then, like I said, my father was in the Army. By that time, I was enjoying school. I was an honor A. I was an A student. I got medals and chains of Honor A, Honor Roll. I do plays 'cause I was interested in acting a lot. Every play that they would do, I would be the first one in line. So I got, in Puerto Rico, I got certificates of Honor A, certificates of the best role-play. I got certificates of everything.

Middle school, I was in Tennessee called Montgomery County, Kenwood Middle School. I was in Tennessee for a couple of years so I did like sixth, seventh, and eighth grades at Kenwood Middle School. I was always the kid that when I was born I couldn't stay still. I was always taking medicine to calm me down. I was always up and moving and that's how I was through middle school and that got me into a lot of trouble. I was always moving, I didn't care. I would never do the work and I started being reckless. That was in Montgomery, that was Kenwood Middle School. It was all right except the problem was that we moved. Once you get used to the school, then the next thing you know you've gotta leave again. That's how my father was. He would never stay still for a certain amount of time.

I was in Puerto Rico by high school and I think I did ninth grade in Tennessee. I'm not sure, but I think I'm positive that ninth grade I did it in Tennessee. That's when I got kicked out of school. I got kicked out of every school in the county. When you start growing up it's like, for me, I didn't want to go to school. There's not really a particular reason. It's just like I wanted to work. I wanted to get money. I wanted to buy my own things so I didn't put mind to school and I'm the type of person that I don't mess around with nobody. But there's always going to be a time when there are one or two knuckleheads that's going to test you. They're going to put you through a test. It's like, I'm a quiet dude. Everywhere I'm quiet and I won't start with nobody. But you put me through the test and people try to make you do something that you don't want to do… well, that was me. I always had to prove myself because everybody trying to hurt me.

When I was back in middle school, everybody tried to pick on me because I was the quiet one and I always answered everything. That's when everybody started picking on me until one day I just got mad and I started fighting a lot. Everybody would pick on me because that school was like people that are not really that smart but they help you. So once you know that you're doing every single work, you get almost a hundred percent and the other people get sixty, seventy or eighty percent. The people that do bad, they look at you like, "Oh, but look at him." Like the mentality of little kids, you know. So I always had to prove myself. They started to try and get on me, you know, so I started fighting and then I got suspended. I kept on fighting, got expelled. I went to an alternative school, which is for kids that get kicked out of their regular school because of whatever reason. I got kicked out of the alternative school.

My parents got mad because I was doing so good. Instead of me ignoring the people around me, I will go with them. Like I said, I never stay still. But when it comes to school, I do my work but after I finish the work, the teacher would go over it and I wouldn't care because I know how to do it. I was always in English class and I had Spanish class. Spanish I already knew 'cause I know how to write, talk, speak. I know how to do everything in

Spanish, and I'm good in English. I'm good in a lot of subjects that I like. The only problem is probably my reading. Back then, my reading... and it's not even reading 'cause I can read. It's comprehending... how the quotations, punctuations, and all that work. That was the hardest part for me 'cause I can read and write English. I can write you a sentence but if there are commas within that sentence I wouldn't know where to put them.

In middle school, I got close to maybe two friends because it's like my mother always told me, "Don't trust everybody that's around you because the first person that's going to put you into deep trouble could be one of your friends." When I was in middle school, I would always go to my mother and say, "Oh, he's my best friend," this and that and she would always tell me, "Don't trust everybody," 'cause your best friend could put you in a danger that you don't want to be in. Your best friend would be somebody that gives you ideas not to go down the wrong path, will stand beside you, is not doing bad himself, you know, is going through the right way and will try to put you through the right way. That's what a friend would be.

THE FUTURE

I haven't gone to school here in New York. I enrolled in a GED program but they said that the GED program is going to be like two and a half years or whatever their reasons may be. So I signed up but I ain't never went. I never went to school.

What I want for the future is I want to go to college. I mean, the first step is complete my GED, which I'm happy about because I was going to quit the school. I was going to quit because two times I took the entire test and both times I got the same score. I took it again the third time and I got a higher score. So now I need three more points—one point for the reading and two points for the math—in order for me to take the predictors. Predictors I heard is kind of easy, so I'm hoping that I take the predictor, I pass the predictor, then next month I should be able to take my GED test. You know, I've gotta start with my GED.

After I get my GED, I want to try to go to college. I got some information, some people that's helping me try to enroll. I'm already enrolled in CUNY Catch. They already did the papers and everything. So when I get out, all I've gotta do is report to CUNY Catch and they already got everything settled for us. I want to do business administration. I want my own business. To tell you the truth, that's what I want to do. I want my own business. I want to own my own restaurant or my own clothing store. I want something of my own. I want to see if I can manage a business.

EVERYTHING IS NOT ABOUT MONEY: LEARN FROM ME

Well, everything is not about money. It's not about how you do things. You can be as real as you can be, you can get as much money as you can, but there's going to come a time and a point where it's going to go downhill. Let's say you making money and you sell it and you selling it big time. You're making money. Well, in all reality you look at the consequences behind that. You are either going to end up dead or you are going to end up in jail. So try to stop if you can. Some people listen to that and they'd be like, "Oh, I'm not stopping getting money." But it's going to come to a time and place where some bad experience is going to happen to you. Just don't let it be you and don't let it get to the point where you're going to lose somebody that you really love because of your actions. Or you're going to lose everything that you love because of your actions.

It's not all about money. Right now, I'm 21 years old and now I'm starting to get my GED. I've been out of school for five years, six years out of school. So it's like, yeah, money… you get money. It's not all about money because you can have as much money as you can have but all that really don't go with you. It's better to get your GED. Once you get your

GED, it's cool and you've gotta succeed. The only hard part is the school but once you get out of school and you've got that Bachelors or you've got that degree right in front of you, you gonna be making twenty dollars or somethin' an hour. Or you're going to be making $30 an hour, depending on what you want to do. That's more than getting paid five hundred a week, or a thousand… two or three thousand a week on a block. One day, it's going to add up to more. Why? Because you don't gotta worry that the man that's next to you going to try to kill you for your money. You go buy something—you go buy kilos or something with twenty thousand—you don't know if they gonna stick you up. You don't know if they gonna kill you for your twenty. It's like you ain't gotta worry about none of that, paranoid, none of that all that. The only thing that you gotta worry about is you getting up in the morning, go to your job, handle your job, do what your job gotta do, come back home to your wife, your kids, whatever the case may be. It's like you will get something good out of it if you go to school.

I'm just trying to push myself now into taking my GED and going to college. I want my Bachelors degree. I'm going to go study for business administration, and I want that to be done. Little by little, it's probably another five years before I get my papers and I get everything the way I want it to be. But after those five years 'til you die you gonna be making a lot more money than you would working in the street for five years, and the sixth year you get killed. So what does that add up to? That doesn't add up to nothing. At least after you're 25 years old until you die, you're gonna be getting money the legal way.

I found out the hard way. To tell you the truth, I've had more experience than anybody else has, some that I can't really talk about, so there's a lot that I've been through. I really don't have no regrets because I knew what I was doing. All this time I knew what I was doing. So regret is something that you wouldn't want, in other words saying, "Oh, you don't know what you're doing." "Oh, I regret doing this." You know what I'm saying? Or, "I regret doing that."

To tell you the truth, I really don't have no regrets. Why? Because when the money was there, it was nice. The money was there, I had a big life. My life was good, so what's the regret if you enjoy the money that you have?

For the people that might be reading the story or listening to whatever I have to say, try to switch your life. Try to change your life before it's too late. Don't be a fool just 'cause you're blinded by the money you get, 'cause I was blinded by the money I was getting. I was making money, but it's not all about the money, like I've said. Try to change your life before it's too late or before anything happens to one of your family members and then it's too late for you to go to school, go to college, or do what you really want to do 'cause deep down inside you don't want to be a big-time drug dealer. Some people might hope for it, but then you are just looking at getting murdered. Just think of it like that. Just try to do good, try to switch your whole life around because, trust me, it will help you on the long run, you know what I'm saying?

God will forgive me so it's just like sometimes I pray to God. I talk to Him. I do my little prayers here and there and I say them. But the main thing I say, "I'm sorry. I know it was my fault. I knew what I was doing. I'm sorry." So one day, He will forgive me for this.